ABBA! FATHER!

ABBA! FATHER!

A PERSONAL CATECHISM

Gerald O'Mahony

CROSSROAD · NEW YORK

1982

The Crossroad Publishing Company
575 Lexington Avenue, New York, NY 10022

Copyright © St Paul Publications 1981

Printed in the United States of America

Library of Congress Catalog Card Number:

ISBN: 0-8245-0546-8
ISBN: 0-8245-0519-0 pbk

PREFACE

In my various attempts at housekeeping, I have discovered that there are bad ways, good ways and better ways of folding up clothes. A garment that appears quite complicated and untidy can be made to look even clumsier, or tidy, or very neat, depending on the way it is folded up for packing away or for ironing.

Using this as a metaphor, I would say that the formal instruction I was given in the Catholic faith in my childhood, following *A Catechism of Christian Doctrine*, gave me that faith folded up in the wrong places, so much so that the whole message was distorted in my mind and heart. As the years went by, and further instruction was added to prayer and experience on the journey towards being a Jesuit and a priest, one by one I began to see the doctrines of the Church in a new light, from new angles.

The trouble then was, the new way of looking at one part of the faith did not match up with the old way of looking at all the other parts of the faith. In other words, I had discovered the first clues to an entirely different way of folding up the same garment, and the new way seemed to suit the garment better than the old way.

I have not been alone in the discovery, and this little book presenting the new way I look at the old truths is but one among hundreds of similar personal catechisms that have appeared in the past twenty years. Where it differs from the others is that it is written in simpler language than most, and is a lot shorter than most. For that reason, it may help a less specialised readership of people, parents and teachers, adult Catholics who like myself have lived through times of great change in the Church but who have not had as much time as I have been given for praying and reading and thinking things through. Also, readers will find that I think in pictures, not in definitions, which makes another difference between this and most other recent popular statements of faith.

The trouble with the *Catechism of Christian Doctrine* lay especially in the structure of the book, where the hinges of the argument were put. In the summary on the flyleaf of the catechism, the inner structure was made quite clear. Faith, Hope, Charity and The Sacraments were the titles of the four main sections, and the way they linked together was given in the answer to question 8: *To save my soul I must worship God by Faith, Hope and Charity; that is, I must believe in Him, I must hope in Him, and I must love Him with my whole heart.*

I was, apparently, here to save my soul. So therefore, I *must* believe the twelve articles of the Apostles' Creed (questions 13-134); I *must* have good works (question 135) and Hope, which meant I *must* pray for it (qq. 135-143) chiefly by the *Our Father* and the *Hail Mary* (qq. 144-168); I *must* love God by keeping his commandments (qq. 169-227) and the commandments of the Church (qq. 228-248). I *must* frequent the Sacraments (qq. 249-312) as a means of expressing Hope and getting the grace to keep the commandments. As an appendix, then came short chapters on Virtues and Vices (qq. 313-332), The Christian's Rule of Life (qq. 333-354) and The Christian's Daily Exercise (qq. 355-370).

The way it came over, to me and to countless others of my generation, was as 370 things I must do to save my soul.

The Good News was absolutely nowhere. Faith, prayer and the sacraments were all turned into hidden commandments, and the commandments, all of them, were compulsory if I was to be saved.

*   *   *

There is a story about a history student who was preparing for a big examination. He did as his tutor suggested, and got all his notes on all the likely essays down to one page of notes per essay. Then he whittled the notes down to one postcard of notes per essay. Then he put the key points of all the essays together on just one page. Then he reduced the one page to one sentence. Then he summed up the sentence in one word. Now all he had to do was to go in to the examination remembering the one word, and from that one word he would be able to recall all the rest. Unfortunately, he got into the examination hall and could not for the life of him recall the one word!

Suppose we were asked to reduce our whole faith to one word, what would the one word be? To my way of thinking, there is only one possible answer: "*Abba!*". If you read on, you will find out why. From this word everything else depends. As a pebble is thrown into a pond and the ripples spread ever further in widening circles, so everything in our christian faith spreads out from "*Abba!*"

My favourite nursery rhyme as a child was *The house that Jack built*:

> This is the house that Jack built
>
> This is the malt
> that lay in the house that Jack built
>
> This is the rat

that ate the malt
that lay in the house that Jack built . . .

and so on, each new verse including only one new feature,
then repeating all the previous verses. The final verse
has twelve features, but they all come back to the house
that Jack built:

This is the horse and the dog and the horn
that belonged to the farmer sowing his corn
that kept the cock that crowed in the morn
that woke the priest all shaven and shorn
that married the man all tattered and torn
that kissed the maiden all forlorn
that milked the cow with the crumpled horn
that tossed the dog
that worried the cat
that killed the rat
that ate the malt
that lay in the house that Jack built.

The reader will find that the statement of faith in this
book keeps doubling back on itself in a similar fashion,
and at the heart of it is the house that Jesus built, on
the rock of his Father's love for us.

CONTENTS

THE GOOD NEWS

"Abba!"

"Abba!" means "Father!" "Abba!" is not just a word written about somebody, but a name spoken to somebody. The heart of the christian message is not a statement about God, but a name spoken out loud.

There is a difference between "Abba!" and "Father!" "Abba!" was, and still is in Hebrew-speaking families, a special name given by children to their father: it is a name which only belongs inside the family. In our families, we have each our own way of calling the father of the family. For my own family it was "Daddy!", for others it is "Dad!" or "Pops!" or any number of alternatives. The only way to get the full flavour of "Abba!" is to ask yourself, what did you call your own father in your own family circle as a child? Then call God by that name.

If you had no father to love, then call God by the name you would have given the father you always longed for as a child.

●

Jesus, Son of God

Who speaks the word, "Abba!"?

Jesus of Nazareth was the one who taught us to call God "Abba!" (Whenever you read "Abba!", translate the word into your own family's intimate name for

3

your father. There is no point in my actually calling God *"Abba!"* if "Daddy!" for me means what *"Abba!"* meant for Jesus. For me to call God *"Abba!"* would be for me to use a foreign word and maybe miss the whole point.)

Before Jesus was born, nobody in the history of the world, so far as we can discover, ever dared to call God *"Abba!"* ("Daddy!", "Dad!", "Da!", "Pops!" "Father!", ... use your own word, not mine). God was known as the father of all creation, the father of the Jewish people, along with many other titles, but nobody seems to have taken that way of speaking to its logical conclusion and called God *"Abba!"* There is all the difference in the world between saying "God is like a father" and standing up, looking towards God and saying *"Abba!"* The difference may not appear so enormous, to us looking back. We have had, after all, two thousand years to get used to the novelty. But in all the countless centuries of the history of man before Jesus of Nazareth, nobody ever dared to call God "Father!" using the intimate family name to his face.

Jesus of Nazareth did dare, and he taught his followers to do the same.

●

The Gospel, the Good News

The word "gospel" means "Good News". The Good News brought by Jesus of Nazareth was "You can call God *'Abba!'* "

That was news to the human race. Perhaps people had wondered; many had come close to the knowledge. Nobody had arrived at the knowledge, until Jesus arrived with the news.

This news was his whole message. Jesus of Nazareth was a prophet, a man with a strong sense of vocation. He himself knew God as *"Abba!"*, and prayed always like that, and he saw the enormous gulf between his way of praying and the way the rest of the world prayed and had always prayed.

The news was so good. At one stroke it wiped away all the sin of the world, past, present and to come. The one we call *"Abba!"* ("Father!", "Daddy!" . . .) loves us not because we are good children, but because we are his children. Jesus invites us to ask ourselves: "Why did my parents love me? Why do I love my own children? Do I love them with strings attached, on condition that they please me first, or do I love them for nothing, freely, just for being my children?" The answer every parent worth the name will give, is that he or she loves the children for nothing. In most cases, the more disappointing the children turn out to be, the greater the reserves of love parents will summon up.

So sin is conquered. No matter how much I disappoint God, he will never love me less for it, but if anything rather more.

From the beginning of time, man had been puzzling and searching, how to keep on the right side of the Mystery of life. Jesus solved the puzzle by saying, "You do not have to try, only to trust. God loves you for nothing, quite freely, the way good parents love their children".

An immense weight, an immense burden drops off the shoulders of the human race — if the Good News is true.

●

The Spirit

The Spirit is "the spirit of adoption, by which we cry out *'Abba!*, Father!' ", as St Paul twice tells us (Galatians 4:6 and Romans 8:15). Hearing the Good News is not immediately enough for sinful man. The burden only finally drops from his shoulders when he gets into the spirit of Jesus, when he "gets the hang" of calling God "Father!" and sees God as Jesus sees him. Or we could say, the burden only finally drops from man's shoulders when the spirit of Jesus gets into him.

The Spirit comes gradually. When we learn to swim, to roller-skate, to skate on ice, to play a musical instrument, and the more crucial art of getting on with one another, we experience breakthroughs along the way. Even in human arts, after the big breakthrough when we feel we have mastered the art, there is always something else to learn, there are always refinements and further horizons to dream of. So it is with the gift of calling God *"Abba!"* The wonderful truth does not hit us all at once, though there are special moments when it dawns on us as never before. For someone who grew up accustomed to be scared of God, the first deep realisation that God is incurably friendly can be quite overwhelming. Even after we have lived with the truth in peace for many years, we find corners of our lives where the light has not yet penetrated. And, naturally, the Spirit cannot enlighten my old age until I reach old age.

Jesus apparently spoke of the Spirit as "he", called him "the Counsellor", and promised to send him, or to send him from God, or that God would send him.

The Spirit is our Defence Counsel or Advocate in court. When we are on trial (as we always are) because of our crimes, shortcomings, failures, omissions and generally disappointing showing as human beings, the court demands to know what we have to say for ourselves. Whereupon the Spirit in us turns to God and makes us cry out *"Abba! Father!"*, which renders the court powerless to condemn us.

The Spirit is also the spirit of truth. The truth that matters is not the truth of our human sins and short-

6

comings, but the more powerful truth of God's bottomless store of patience and forgiveness. The truth that God has for us a parent's love overrides all other truths.

God's justice is the same as his mercy. God's idea of justice is to have mercy. "Lord, you reveal your mighty power most of all by your forgiveness and compassion . . .", as the Prayer of the Church reminds God (Prayer of the 26th Week of the Year).

●

Adoption

The Spirit is the spirit of adoption. We are each of us and all of us God's children, but by adoption. Jesus of Nazareth is the only one we call God's own Son, the "only-begotten".

We can truly call God *"Abba!* Father!", but it was Jesus who taught us. It was Jesus who gave us the courage to reverse millions of years of lack of trust in the Mystery of life. So far as we can tell, nobody taught Jesus: calling God *"Abba!"* came naturally to him. The gospel of Luke shows Jesus at the age of twelve referring to God as "my Father", and the adult Jesus has built up a whole life-style and vocabulary and system of stories and teachings around the central notion of "Come to God as your own Father".

Here is surely the best way in, not only to the mystery of God but also to the mystery of Jesus as God the Son. I am God's son by adoption, by courtesy of Jesus. He is God's Son by courtesy of his Father, naturally. I would never have learnt to call God "Father!" but for Jesus.

The Spirit was present in Jesus always. There was no time when Jesus was without the Spirit. He knew too much about God, ever to have learned it from others. Whenever his enemies attacked him, it was the Spirit who answered in him; he spoke up completely in character, in complete

7

harmony with one who prays *"Abba! Father!"* to God. In Jesus of Nazareth alone the Spirit was not a spirit of adoption, but was his own spirit. He did not read his answers off from anywhere, but spoke straight from his heart secrets about God which had been hidden from countless ages.

We, too, when our faith is challenged, do not have to worry about how to answer, since the Spirit speaks up for us. But in us the Spirit is present by courtesy of Jesus.

●

Crucifixion: Was Jesus right?

The Good News was the best news ever to fall on human ears — if it was true. In the presence of Jesus of Nazareth, many disciples and friends and crowds of listeners were, so the gospels tell us, able to believe that the news was true. Many of the listeners, though, were not at all sure that the news was true, or good, or from God.

There were the nationalists, who were convinced that God was planning to overthrow the Roman conquerors and set Israel free. How could Jesus be the Christ, the promised, anointed leader commissioned by God, if he refused to be made king, spoke out against violence, and openly fraternised with Roman officers?

There were the self-righteous, who were convinced that the way to heaven and the way to gain God's favour was to keep the law of Moses, and the traditions, perfectly. How could Jesus be the Christ from God, if he announced that for anyone the best approach to God is to call him *"Abba! Father!"*? In that case, sinners would get away with being sinners; foreigners stood as much chance of God's favour as Israelites; the blind, the lame, the deaf, the lepers, the paralysed, the possessed all had as much right to call God *"Abba!"* as the rich and the prosperous who

8

enjoyed God's blessings. Not content with preaching such a scandalous doctrine, Jesus acted it out, associating as he did with all kinds of sinners: prostitutes, tax collectors, thieves, foreigners, the blind, the lame, the deaf, the lepers, the paralysed and the possessed. In the end Jesus even shared a criminal's execution, and yet he never backed down from his assertion that God was his Father, and that everyone else could follow him in calling God "Abba! Father!"

There were the worldly, the Establishment figures, who may genuinely have thought that Roman rule was the best thing for the nation, with themselves as a puppet government. They were afraid that Jesus could cause a rising in spite of himself, and bring down on Jerusalem the might of Rome, to destroy the nation beyond hope of recovery.

Then there were the Romans themselves, for whose Empire the Eastern Mediterranean countries had always been a thorn in the side. They were very sensitive about large gatherings, as every army of occupation has always been and always will be. They were bound to be nervous about this man people were calling king.

Eventually his enemies united, and put Jesus on trial. They put him to death, and for Jesus' followers that meant the Good News was false news. They still thought that God always blesses his favourites with prosperity, so it was preposterous to think that God would let his favoured son die a criminal's death. Jesus had obviously been too daring, and God had dropped him. The enemies of Jesus, too, thought that they had effectively squashed the Good News, and all the trouble it was generating.

●

Resurrection: Yes, Jesus was right

When the apostles and other disciples saw Jesus risen again on the third day and subsequently, they saw him in such a way that only God could have showed him to them.

9

"God has raised this man Jesus, whom you crucified",
was the way Peter proclaimed the resurrection to the
crowds in Jerusalem (e.g., Acts 2:23f.). Not only the fact
that Jesus was personally alive and present to them, but
the very manner of his being shown to them spoke, to
Peter and the other witnesses, of the power of God and
no other. This was no ordinary seeing.

We might say that the very first joy at the resurrection,
before the minds of the witnesses got to work on the
consequences, was a personal joy: Jesus whom they had
loved so well and for whom they had given up everything,
was now risen beyond death.

Then the logical conclusion that eventually struck them was
that "Jesus was right about God, after all. Otherwise God
would not have vindicated him like this, raising him in glory
and serenity, infinitely beyond the reach of his enemies.
Jesus must have been right, when he called God *Abba!*
Father!' and taught us to do the same. The Good News
is true".

●

Pentecost

The conclusion took time to dawn. We could well think
of Pentecost as the day it dawned on the witnesses that
the Good News was true and irreversible, the day when
it dawned on them all how to call God "*Abba!* Father!",
the day they acquired the gift, the "know-how" . . . the
Spirit.

●

The Ascension

In the resurrection of Jesus, he appeared to the witnesses
as alive and glorified.

He was alive, personally the same Jesus they had known in the flesh, but completely transformed. It was as if he was now at God's right hand. To get an impression of what this "right hand" means, we can think back to the story of the patriarch Joseph.

Joseph was the dreamer, the son of Jacob, his father's favourite who made all his brothers jealous. They sold him into slavery in Egypt, but there he rose to be the Pharaoh's right hand man. The Pharaoh then seemed to stand back and say to his people: "If you want anything from me, go to Joseph. If I want to tell you anything, you will hear it through Joseph" (cf. Genesis 41:55).

The memory that the resurrection appearances left with the witnesses was that God had put Jesus in much the same position with regard to himself as the Pharaoh once did with Joseph. God was now saying, "If you want anything from me, go to Jesus. If I want to tell you anything, you will hear it through Jesus".

Another great impression left particularly by the latest of the appearances of Jesus was, "He will come again. The glory and power he has now, the glory I could see when last I saw him, is so much greater and more real than the glory of the sun, that I am quite sure he will come back again. If he has withdrawn, it is for good reasons of his own. Nor has he forgotten me, since I was the reason for all his grief and joy".

The first and essential thing that Jesus passes on to us from God's right hand is the Good News. "Welcome to the court of the king, my brothers. See, my dreams came true: you are my brothers, and God is pleased that I call him 'Abba!' I was right, wasn't I?".

●

Hope

The traditional symbol for hope is an anchor. Jesus is my hope, because I am like a boat, and he is like my anchor firmly fixed on the shore at the right hand of God, but tied to me by bonds of brotherhood.

Hope is closely connected to the ascension of Jesus. Those who see Jesus risen and know him alive in the resurrection are not dismayed when the clouds hide him from their vision again. The power and the glory that they saw is immeasurably brighter than the power and glory of daylight, and the witnesses know that it is only a matter of time until Jesus returns. They know he is there with his Father and our Father, but tied to us as a brother. All his sweat and blood was, in God's providence, for our sake, so he is not going to forget us now. The meetings with Jesus in the resurrection were personal meetings, convincing the witnesses that Jesus' memory of them was still very much alive, in Jesus alive. His memory was part of himself as it always had been. We need only think of the way Peter was forgiven for his denials, and the way Mary Magdalene knew she was being called by name in the garden.

Others, besides the witnesses to the resurrection who had known Jesus in the flesh, can be shown Jesus alive. St Paul on the road to Damascus can be thought of as the first, but he was not the last. What makes the witness of those who knew Jesus in the flesh so uniquely precious is the fact that they recognised in the risen Jesus the same person they had known in the flesh. From then on, all he had said, all he had done was sealed with the glory of God — especially, the way he had called God *"Abba!* Father!" and lived accordingly.

Jesus is my anchor; the shore in which the anchor is bedded is God's fatherly love for me.

●

The earliest creed

The earliest versions of what we know as the creed were very simple: *Jesus is the Christ, the Son of God,* or else *Jesus is the Christ, the Lord.* The gospels generally use the first way of speaking; St Paul generally prefers the second. Every time Paul speaks of *the Lord Jesus Christ,* or *Christ Jesus the Lord,* or *Jesus Christ the Lord,* he is expressing his faith in the creed.

If we believe that *Jesus is the Christ* (which is the first half of both versions of the creed), we are saying that he is the Messiah, the anointed one, the saviour promised by God and long-awaited, the last word, the real truth, genuinely sent by God, with a genuine vocation to say what he said.

What did he say? What was the saving fulfilment of the promise, the last word, the real truth? He said, "You can call God *'Abba! Father!'* and trust him as a child trusts a loving parent".

If we believe that *Jesus is the Son of God,* we trust his instinct about the Fatherhood of God, as being the testimony of one who *knows.* I see that here is one who speaks from the inside of a very special relationship which I never would have dreamed of unless he, the Son, had shown me; but once he has shown me, I can recognise in myself the truth of what he shows me.

If we believe that *Jesus is the Lord,* we are saying in effect the same as when we affirm that Jesus is the Son of God, with extra overtones of glory and power and "right hand of God", since Lord as used in this creed is a divine title previously reserved to God.

Looking back, we can feel today that the two halves of the early creed seem to amount to the same thing. The difference was more real to the apostles and disciples. They had expected a Messiah, and Peter and a few others were inspired to see this promised Messiah (Christ, God's

13

anointed leader) in Jesus of Nazareth, before ever the real depths of God's mercy had fully dawned on them. To one living in darkness, there are two stages. First, here is some-one sent from God, on whom I can stake everything. Second, this saviour is inviting me to treat myself as a child of God.

The creed, then, is not ousting the Father from the central position in christianity. On the contrary, to believe that Jesus is the Christ, the Son of God means to believe and trust in God as our Father. We believe it on the strength of Jesus, but we believe it of the Father.

"We believe in Jesus Christ the Son of God" means "We believe that we can call God 'Abba! Father!'".

BAPTISM:

CELEBRATING THE GOOD NEWS

Baptism

Baptism is the ceremony by which we christians celebrate the fact that we are children of God by adoption. All children born into the world are children of God, did they but know it. Christians are those who do know, thanks to Jesus of Nazareth, and we celebrate the entry of each new believer into the community by baptism.

The ceremony was chosen by Jesus himself, so the gospel records tell us. He himself went through a ceremony of baptism, being baptised by John the Baptiser in the River Jordan. According to Mark's gospel, when Jesus came up out of the water from John's baptism, "he saw the heavens opened and the Spirit descending upon him like a dove; and a voice came from heaven, 'You are my beloved Son; with you I am well pleased' " (Mark 1:10f.). His baptism is a model of every christian baptism: acting like Jesus, we receive the Spirit of being God's child, and we hear the Father, the voice from heaven, say "You are my beloved child; with you I am well pleased". Each day that follows, even to the end of our lives, God is saying the same thing to us: "You are my beloved child; with you I am well pleased, not for anything you have done or failed to do, but simply because you are my child".

●

The character of baptism

God is not pleased with me because I have deserved it, but simply because he chose me, he loved me and he loves me for ever. His love for me is settled. I am a member of his family, and from now on I shall always have my own place at his table. He counts me in on the "bread of the children". If ever I run away and seek my security elsewhere, he will not forget my name or remove my place from his table, but will always keep it for me as long as I live and beyond the grave.

For that reason, the ceremony of baptism is never repeated with the same person. If a sinner returning to the community had to be baptised again, that would imply that in the meantime God had removed his chair from the table, and told everyone else to move up one place.

●

Baptism: a celebration

Baptism is the celebration of something which is already true. All celebrations are celebrations of something that is already true, otherwise there is no point in celebrating. But the celebration brings home the truth and pins it down in a tangible action or ceremony, in audible words, in one place and time that can be remembered and treasured, lived up to and lived out.

In baptism we celebrate the gift of God. In particular we are celebrating the Fatherhood of God, the gift of himself as the Father of this candidate or this baby, and we are rejoicing to recall that God has already chosen the rest of us as his children. We celebrate too the gift of life and love and all things in the world, whose source we will never fully understand.

Every gift includes the giver. God is present in all his gifts, just as we human beings make ourselves present to one another by making presents to one another.

●

God the creator

In calling God "Father!", Jesus took for granted the belief
of his people that there is one Mystery behind all the
people, animals, plants, minerals and gases in the universe,
and that the Mystery is the source of all, and is good.

What kind of a source did Jesus say the creator is? A
loving, personal, friendly source, whom we will find
quickest by calling him "*Abba!* Father!"

The doctrine of "creation" has mainly to do with the way
we experience all things, including ourselves, as gifts,
here and now. Only when we know the here and now as a
gift do our minds reach back and admit that therefore
everything that came before was a gift, leading up to
now.

The new way that Jesus looked at God the creator meant
that the story of creation as it was then understood had
to be rewritten.

●

Original sin

"Original sin" is the name we give to the state of those
who do not dare to call God "*Abba!* Father!" In all the
centuries before Jesus of Nazareth was born, men carried
the burden of trying to appease the hidden powers of the
universe and never feeling they had succeeded. Human
beings did not know the secret. There seemed to be a key
missing to the "gates of heaven", and human beings felt
locked out.

There are two ways of talking about "gates of heaven" and
what Jesus did for mankind. We can say that he opened
the gates of heaven for us, or we can say that he taught
us to believe that the gates of heaven had never been
shut. They have always been as wide open as a father's

arms are open to receive an erring child . . . but we never dared to believe they were open. Effectively, for someone who is paralysed with fright, open doors are as shut as locked doors, and we were paralysed with fright.

The fault is not God's, who has always been the same, completely trustworthy. The fault has to do with man's freedom being misused by man. Once in the world, suspicion breeds itself: those who do not trust completely cannot love completely, so their children will be less than completely trusting. There seemed to be no exceptions, until the process was reversed by Jesus.

Why call this fear "original sin"? For one thing, so far as we can tell, the fear has always been there from the beginning, the origin, of human beings. The Garden of Eden, the original paradise described in the Book of Genesis, is not so much a statement that things were once perfect, as a pictorial way of saying that man is ill at ease and so far as we know always has been. We dream of being kings, while we are serfs. For another thing, this fear of calling God *"Abba!* Father!" is the origin of all other sins. "I was afraid of you because you are a severe man; you take up what you did not lay down, and reap what you did not sow" (Luke 19:21). Like the man in Jesus' parable of the talents, mankind buried its talent, and reacted to the Mystery as a scolded child towards a harsh school-teacher, as a criminal towards a policeman. It makes no difference if God is in truth a loving Father: so long as a human being lives in fear of being judged by results, that human being is crippled. Any "good deeds" he does are diseased, because they reflect a stern, demanding god, and are thus a form of idolatry.

Traditionally, the first sin and the root of sin is thought of as being pride. Pride and lack of trust are in fact two aspects of the same evil. Pride, and the desire to "be like gods", is rather the way the Old Testament pictures the start of sin, especially in the third chapter of the Book of Genesis. Lack of trust, fear to believe in God's fatherly love for me is the New Testament way of looking at sin. The New Testament description is truer because the picture of God is truer. God, as it turned out, is not in competition with anybody, except for the lowest place.

●

Light

"Again Jesus spoke to them, saying, 'I am the light of the world' " (John 8:12). Jesus is the light because of what dawned on the human race through him: we can call God "*Abba!* Father!"

In the Old Testament we can see the dawn slowly approaching.

> But Zion said, "The Lord has forsaken me,
>   my Lord has forgotten me."
> "Can a woman forget her sucking child,
>   that she should have no compassion
>   on the son of her womb?
> Even these may forget,
>   yet I will not forget you." (Isaiah 49:14f.)

Isaiah has come so close there to the Good News, and yet he is still worlds away. Hosea, too, came very close, speaking of God loving the people as a father loves a son, teaching the baby to walk, bending down and feeding him. Again, for Hosea God is like a husband whose wife is unfaithful, but who still loves her, each and every time she betrays him.

●

The Old Covenant

The Old Testament, the old covenant, amounted to this when it was first expressed: "I will be your God and

21

your king: you will be my subject people. If you keep my laws, I will look after your interests. If you rebel, I shall treat you as enemies".

Moses was inspired to cast the relationship between God and his people in the mould or model of a treaty between the Pharaoh of Egypt and a subject nation in the Egyptian empire of the time. Strictly speaking, once the people of Israel failed to keep the laws, the covenant with God was broken, finished for ever. Some time or other, the covenant was bound to be broken, and indeed was broken many times over. Yet prophet after prophet spoke for God and gave the people "one more chance", until it became clearer and clearer that the covenant needed re-expressing, rethinking, renewing once for all, since the old mould was inadequate to picture the real God. "The days are coming, says the Lord, when I will make a new covenant with the house of Israel. I will put my law within them, and I will write it upon their hearts" (Jeremiah 31:31.33). "A new heart I will give you, and a new spirit I will put within you; and I will take out of your flesh the heart of stone and give you a heart of flesh" (Ezekiel 36:26).

●

The New Covenant

Jesus was the one who introduced the new covenant, the New Testament. The new form of covenant goes like this: God says to every single human being, "I will be your *Abba;* you will be my child". The model for the new covenant had to be something unconditional and ever-lasting. By now it was obvious to Jesus that the old cove-nant had not gone far enough to picture the real love and faithfulness of God. What was needed was an unbreak-able agreement, unilateral from God's side in as much as "once a father, always a father". No matter how many times a child lets a parent down, the parent does not cease to be a parent, and does not disown the child. "And even if these did, I will not disown you" (cf. Psalm 26[27]:10). The child may disown the parent, but this parent's invitation is never closed. The place at the Father's table will always have the child's name on it.

Parents who disown their children are, after all, closing their eyes to the truth. God could never do that.

●

Candle; white christening robe

This was the light that had grown in intensity through the ages until it shone out in Christ. This is the meaning of the Easter candle at the baptism ceremony, from which a candle is lit for the candidate or the infant who is being baptised. Light dawns on the christian, by courtesy of Christ, that he or she can call God "*Abba!* Father!" and trust him accordingly.

The white garment symbolises the same thing. What gives a child glory in the eyes of any parent is the knowledge, "Child, you are mine". What gives a child glory in the eyes of God is God's decision, "Child, you are mine". My garment is white because God in his indulgent love cannot see the stains, only the glory. And if God cannot see the stains, then they no longer exist. God says (we know from Jesus), "You are my beloved child. With you I am well pleased, not because you guarantee to stay out of trouble, but because you are mine and always will be".

The darkness dispelled by the light of Christ is the fear that God is a hard taskmaster, and a stranger.

●

Water of baptism

In the early days of the christian church, the candidates for baptism were totally immersed in the water of baptism. As if crossing a river, they would cast off their old clothes, step down into the water, cross to the other side, come out and be clothed in the new white garment.

The water of this river of baptism can be looked at three ways: it symbolises what we *rise into* as we emerge . . . new life, new growth, the promised land, the well-watered garden; it symbolises trials and tribulations *through which* we travel on our way to God; and it symbolises what we *leave behind*, the enemies who are drowned, the dross and uncleanness that are washed away.

If the candidate has faith in God as his Father, then the celebration constitutes him as a son of God. Jesus was apparently satisfied if he found faith in those who presented a candidate (cf. Mark 2:5), which is reassuring when we think of our custom of baptising infants. There is a new life, because there is a new child, a new relationship which takes root at baptism. The candidate steps out of the river into a new land.

The troubles we go through in our lifetime are part of our baptism, so Jesus taught his disciples. His death was to be an Exodus (Luke 9:31) and a baptism (Mark 10:38) with which his disciples also would be baptised. We learn God's faithfulness in the school of suffering.

The enemies which are drowned? First and foremost, what is drowned is the fear which prevents a man from believing the Good News that God can be called *"Abba! Father!"* and trusted as such. The fear of being different is drowned: black or white, male or female, clever or dull, silent or talkative, English or French, well or sick, blind or sighted, handsome or ugly, rich or poor, fat or thin. God loves me because I am his, not because I have blue eyes. The fear of sin is drowned: not even sin can separate me from the love of God, because however sinful I may be, I am still God's child sinning, so his love for me is still there, and his love is my salvation, stronger than my sin. Like Pharaoh's army in the sea, like the swine in the Lake of Galilee, the enemy forces are drowned. I step out into the promised land. Nothing can separate me from the love of God. I step out a child of God. I leave behind the state of being an orphan. I am born again.

RESPONSE

Morality

"We love, because God first loved us", says St John (1 John 4:19). "In this is love, not that we loved God but that he loved us and sent his Son to be the expiation for our sins" (*ibid.* verse 10).

The first truth which should always be remembered about morality is that being good does not earn us a place in heaven. We do not deserve God's favour by behaving ourselves. He loves us for nothing, because he chooses to and not for any merit of ours. By the same token, God does not stop loving me when I sin. His love and forgiveness is always instantly available, if I can only trust in it.

What, then, is the mainspring of morality? Why should we bother to be good? The obligation to be good comes from an awareness of how good God has been to me. "Father", I say, "you have been so marvellously good to me. What can I do in return?" To which God replies, "My child, be like me. Become as closely like me as you can become".

Morality, "being good", is the way to thank God for his everlasting covenant of love. It is my *Thank you* to a Father who will love me whether I thank him or not. I reach as high as I can, not with any hopes of paying my debt, of raising my Tower of Babel till I can get even with God and step off into heaven on equal terms, but simply to show the world how real is God's love for me, how grateful I am, how free, how unafraid of falling. The prayer after communion in the first week of the year says to the Father: "Help us to thank you by lives of faithful service".

Imagine how well we would all skate on the ice if we had absolutely no fear of hard consequences from falling. In morality the christian has at his disposal such a fearlessness, because he knows his sins were forgiven even while he committed them, and indeed his present and future sins will not separate him from his Father's love, now that he knows the full depth of it. A christian can launch out into bold choices, because he is not afraid of being penalised for wrong choices.

True morality is gratitude. All sin is ingratitude. That is why the original sin is fear of God as a taskmaster. Who can be grateful to one who will consign him to hell for failure? The origin of sin must be removed before gratitude can start.

Original sin is the basic insecurity of having no secure Father, which leads mankind to seek security elsewhere. If a man does not dare to believe that the one Mystery of life is on his side, then he will turn restlessly to one prop after another, only to find they let him down.

●

The Incarnation

How do we know that God is asking us to be like him? Chiefly, from watching and listening to Jesus. Jesus' vocation was not simply to tell us in words what his Father and our Father is like, but also to show us in action what his Father and our Father is like. Once he has told us and shown us, it becomes obvious that the way to please anyone at all is to be like him, and God is no exception. Moreover, "becoming like God" is the most ennobling, enriching and rewarding way any man or woman could spend a lifetime, so, as we would expect, aiming to thank God we succeed only in turning his blessings back on ourselves.

God sends the sun and the rain equally to his friends and his foes. Be like that, says Jesus. You be like that: be as kind to your enemies as to your friends.

God invites all sorts of hobbledehoys to his banquet, people who haven't a chance of ever repaying him. Remember how he chose *you* and invited *you*. So you be like that. When you have a party, invite the people who cannot pay you back. Be like God. Do things for nothing. Don't charge for your services.

All men and women are God's children, and that is his sole reason for loving them. He loves man and woman, slave and freeman, sinner and saint, white and black, child and adult, diseased and sound, Jew and gentile, fellow-countryman and foreigner, believer and non-believer. Let that be your sole reason for loving them also: they are God's children.

Wherever Jesus could see the shape of God, he translated the thought into action. He made visible to us the invisible God. He loved man and woman, slave and free, sinner and saint, white and black, child and adult, diseased and sound, Jew and gentile, Israelite and foreigner, believer and unbeliever. He treated each with respect, because here was a child of God like himself, with the same claim to God's love as he himself had, did they but know it.

Jesus invited to his party the people who could not pay him back. He worked freely, without charging for his services, and he died forgiving his murderers, which is the furthest human love can go. By the time the murderers have repented, if they ever do repent, the victim is dead and can no longer have the wrong put right or compensated for by the wrongdoers. There is no free service to another which can compare with forgiving him as he kills you.

"Greater love has no man than this, that a man lay down his life for his friends" (John 15:13). Jesus laid down his life for his enemies. There could be no clearer picture of the love Jesus said God has for me, than the sight of Jesus of Nazareth dying on the cross, forgiving his murderers. "Father, forgive them; for they know not what they do" (Luke 23:34). Not, "Father, forgive them if they let me go". Not, "Father, forgive them if they repent". Simply, "Father, forgive them now, while they are killing me".

There is the perfect mirror of the God of the Good News. Did not Jesus say, God loves us even in our sins, not because of our sins but because he sees us through glory-coloured spectacles, as his children? "You are my child, my beloved, even while you try to kill me".

*   *   *

"We love, because God first loved us", St John again reminds us (1 John 4:19). So it was, and is, with Jesus: he loved, because his Father first loved him. From the way Jesus loved and loves us all, we can know how completely he himself was loved in the first place. He reveals, first and foremost, God's love for him.

●

Miracles

Jesus was admitted by friends (e.g., Acts 10:38) and foes (Matthew 12:24) alike to be a wonder-worker. His miracles do not so much prove anything about himself, as give his picture of what God is like. Jesus uses the powers he has, as a means of adding another dimension to the word-picture he is building up of God as our Father. Other people have worked wonders, before and after Jesus, but no one has used them quite as Jesus did, like an artist working in an unusual material, to say what God is like.

32

God has no horror of the leper (Mark 1:40-45), no suspicion of the Romans (Matthew 8:5-10) or other foreigners (Mark 7:24-30); God is more concerned with people than with regulations (Mark 3:1-6); God is eager to open the eyes of the blind and to give understanding (Mark 8:22-26), to open the ears of the deaf and free the tongues of the dumb (Mark 7:31-37) so they can hear the Good News and acknowledge Jesus as the Christ, the Son of God. And so on. God is the friend of life and the enemy of death. God forgives sins, and turns death into a mere sleep. The miracles are signs (John 2:11), visible signs of the God we could not see. Those who recognise the God acknowledge the signs.

●

We believe in the forgiveness of sins

There appears to be one condition to the Good News, which is built-in and inescapable. If I accept God's forgiveness of my sins, I must also accept his forgiveness of everyone else's sins. God is not only my Father, he is everyone else's Father as well. The story of the Prodigal Son was told by Jesus for the benefit of those who made a habit of judging others. The story invites the hearer to step into the shoes of the prodigal's elder brother, and think hard and long before he makes the final decision.

At the end of the story, the father is inviting the elder son into the party being thrown for the returned wastrel. We are not told by Jesus whether the elder brother decides to join his father in forgiving, and to take part in the festivities, or whether he decides to boycott the whole proceedings (Luke 15:32). Jesus cannot tell us the end of the story, because in each case the end of the story depends on the listener's choice, your choice and my choice. If the listener is willing to forgive everyone else that God forgives (that is to say, everyone), then the elder brother joins the merrymaking. If the listener cannot tolerate to

33

share heaven and God's pleasure with those he himself despises, then the elder brother chooses the darkness outside.

The saying of Jesus, "Judge not, and you shall not be judged" thus points to the one danger of all dangers to watch. The God of the Good News, *Abba*, our Father, cannot welcome two brothers or sisters if they cannot bear one another, if they are mutually exclusive. He cannot have two parties, one for the prodigals and one for the self-righteous. He can only be present at one party. There is only one God. If we choose to object to any of our fellow guests, then we are shutting ourselves out.

This life, now, is God's party. This life, now, is when the elder brother makes up his mind. This life, now, is when God is showing us who our fellow guests are. If they are good enough for our host, they had better be good enough for us. We should be very careful not to say to our host, "Either this one goes from here, or I go".

God will forgive us seven times in the day, seventy-seven times in the day if we ask him. But we for our part must be prepared to try and forgive one another seven times in the day, seventy-seven times, every time. My salvation will not depend on whether I succeed, in my own eyes, in forgiving my enemies, but it might depend on whether I have wanted and tried to forgive them. Forgiving others is not a burden. Judging others is the burden, and Jesus begs us to drop it, and take up his burden instead, which is the sweet and light one of forgiving and being forgiven.

We have had an immense load taken off us by having all our sins and ingratitude forgiven. All Jesus asks, for our own good, is that we do not put the burden on our fellow guests by reminding them of their debts to us. We would then become a stumbling-block to them, making it harder for them to believe in the generosity of their host, instead of making his generosity clearer to them.

If we condemn others for their sins and demand retribution from them, then we have put a taskmaster god back in heaven; in that case we have shouldered the burden of retribution for ourselves as well, since *that* god never forgave us (cf. Matthew 18:23-35).

●

Brotherly love

Because we have all of us one Father, we are all brothers and sisters. Our relationship with one another does not depend on our being all of the one human family; it depends, for a christian, on our equal status as sons and daughters of the one Father. If I can call God *"Abba!"* and you can call God *"Abba!"*, and therein lies our greatest glory, then neither of us can boast above the other.

The animals, plants and minerals of the universe also have God for Father, but they do not know him as *"Abba!"*. For their voice to praise God consciously, they depend upon mankind in whom they are taken up. When we praise God, minerals and chemicals find a voice to praise him in our bodies; plant life praises him, and the animal kingdom praises him, for we are plant and we are animal. When we praise God and call him *"Abba!"*, the whole universe starts to speak with the one voice of Christ. We humans are the crown of the universe, but Christ is the crown of humankind.

The christian conscience must have to do with "one world". All men and women are brothers and sisters. The resources of the universe belong to each one as much as they belong to any other; we can never rightly rest as long as one nation goes hungry while another has too much to eat; we can never rightly rest as long as one generation exploits the irreplaceable resources of the earth at the expense of future generations.

Jesus called us brothers and sisters of his, thinking not just of his own generation but of all who lived before him and of all who might come after him. St Paul spoke of mankind as being cells or members of the one body (cf. 1 Corinthians 12:12ff.). St John preferred the image of the one vine with many branches (cf. John 15:5). St Peter, perhaps thinking of the meaning ("rock") of the name Jesus had given him, referred to the unity to be built up as a living temple of God, each of us being living stones (cf. 1 Peter 2:5). Jesus also spoke of one flock with one shepherd (cf. John 10:16). The Jews already thought of themselves as one nation with one father, Israel, and one leader, Moses, even though there were twelve tribes within the nation. Jesus took over the image of the twelve tribes with his Twelve apostles, but made the nation a universal kingdom. One city, one temple, one God.

●

Spirit of unity

The Spirit, as well as being the spirit of adoption, is the spirit of unity. Because we all call God *"Abba!* Father!" we are all one family. Because God loves each one equally and for ever, we must be a unified family, endlessly forgiving of one another.

Jesus is the head, the leader, the shepherd, the cornerstone, the helmsman, the fisherman, because he is the one who first taught the rest of us to say *"Abba!* Father!" His Spirit unites us.

His Spirit's special care is the forgiveness of sins. When God adopted me, he forgave my sins. When God adopts us — not just me, but us — then the Spirit urges me to forgive my brothers and sisters as often as God will forgive me, which is to say, every time they offend me.

The Spirit is my Counsel for the Defence when I am on trial. But if I base my defence on calling God *"Abba!"*,

I must be prepared to hear the judge reply, "Then take your foot off the neck of your brother, please. His defence is the same as yours".

God will forgive us our sins, if we drop the charges against one another.

●

Incarnation today

Jesus showed us what the invisible God looks like. To see him, was to see the Father. To hear him, was to hear what God has to say. The Word that God wanted to tell us was "made flesh" in Jesus, took on flesh and blood so we could see it and hear it and follow it.

The Incarnation did not stop there. If Jesus' hearers and watchers followed his way, they would first "be converted", that is, learn to call God "Abba!", and thus have all their sins forgiven. Then, in gratitude, as a *Thank you,* they would imitate God as Jesus had done. They would translate the word of God in *their* flesh, in *their* lives, in *their* turn. Even though the day should come when Jesus in the flesh was no longer to be seen on earth, future generations would have others to look at, in whom God would be made flesh in the same Spirit, and on the same pattern, as was seen in Jesus.

You and I, followers of Christ, are invited to look at God and then to become God for our generation "My brothers and sisters, you say you cannot see God. Look at me, if you wish to know what God is like". Such a claim sounds blasphemous at first, but is not that what the disciples of Jesus are supposed to be and to do and to say? A christian does not have to be sinless to reflect God as Father. The prodigal sons among us give the world a far better account of what God is really like than the righteous but unbending. So long as the gathering of disciples has forgiveness in its very bones, it can still magnify the Lord.

We can express this vocation of ours in different ways but still mean the same thing. "Be like your Father in heaven" means "Be like Jesus", because Jesus is the perfect image of his Father. Like father, like son. God in the Old Testament writings is the shepherd. Jesus is the shepherd in the New Testament, then Peter is the shepherd, and the church of Jesus' followers is a shepherd to the world, so you and I become shepherds. God is the rock ("my rock, my refuge, my stronghold") in the psalms, Jesus is the rock in the New Testament, then Simon is called Cephas ("Peter", "rock") by Jesus; the church is a rock; you and I are living stones.

God is the rock on whom we can rely when all else fails. Wise men, therefore, put their feet on the rock well before the floods come, and do all their building there. Jesus is the rock because he tells us how to plant ourselves on God in such a way as never to be shaken off the rock. "Call God 'Abba!'. Trust him like that. Then you will find the everlasting covenant. Then you will find everlasting life". Peter is the rock first and foremost because he was the first to whom God revealed that Jesus was his chosen messenger. Nor would Peter ever forget what it meant to call God "Abba!", and to be forgiven, because he had been forgiven by the risen Christ. The church is the rock because it holds out the same hope, teaches the same secret about God. You and I are the rock, are living stones, insofar as we show an unshakable trust in God's mercy and friendliness, insofar as we call God "Abba!" and trust him like that. Others will come to us for security, be built in above us. We shall feel their weight.

God is light. Jesus is the light of the world. And, says Jesus to us his disciples, "You are the light of the world". Jesus is the light because he first taught us how to approach God. We are the light of the world, because having once learnt the way to approach God, we in our turn become a beacon and a lighthouse for the guidance of others.

38

All the images of God to be found in the scriptures can be applied to Jesus, but also to Peter and the church, and finally to you and me, members of the church.

"May we come to share in the divinity of Christ, who humbled himself to share in our humanity". The divine characteristics become yours and mine.

●

The Way

"Be like God. Jesus is the perfect image of God, so be like Jesus".

The early followers of Christ were known as Followers of the Way before ever they were known as christians. Two of the gospels, Mark and Luke, make a central theme out of *the way* that Jesus walked to Jerusalem and to his death; John's gospel gives us Jesus saying "I am the Way". The Way was known as the way of the cross right from the start. Followers of Christ must take up their cross daily and follow him to Calvary. Simon of Cyrene was instantly recognised and then remembered as the perfect picture of a disciple.

The Way is nothing other than Jesus' way of calling God *"Abba!* Father!"* and trusting him accordingly, then trying to be like him. The world provides the cross.

The journey is not a purely physical journey, the steps we take on our daily round. The journey is a spiritual journey, from being like Adam and Eve in the story to being just like God. Jesus is the one who shows us the way "back into paradise", by walking through the gates to show they are open, and forgiving all fellow travellers. Jesus praises the unjust steward in his own story, who tore up the owner's bills and made them smaller. That is the way to get on in the kingdom. The meetings between Jesus and his fellow human beings are our guide to how we should treat our fellows today.

•

Conscience

When Jesus spoke about his Father's will, he was speaking about the call present in his own conscience. We need not be surprised at Jesus' seeming lack of references to conscience, for he was constantly referring to it, under the name of his Father's will. He even referred to it as his food: "My food is to do the will of him who sent me" (John 4:34).

This is not to belittle either the conscience of Jesus or his relationship with his Father's will. We cannot say that the will of Jesus' Father was "only his conscience". His conscience was for Jesus, as my conscience is for me, the means by which the Father communicates his will.

Conscience is my judgement about the action in front of me. Conscience is the gap between "me as I am" and "me as I could be". I am constantly challenged to be the person I could be, to be like God, to put God into flesh in my life, to choose the line of action which will show God most clearly to the world, which will give God the greater glory.

God calls me every day in the things I have to do, and in the alternative things I could perhaps do if I had the courage. The thought that there are alternatives makes me restless, since there are times when I feel I could change the world, and other times when I feel weak and helpless and tied in by my own diffidence and the habits I have formed, scarcely able to cope with the limited responsibility I have already taken on.

The most consoling thought of all is that behind my conscience is forgiveness. If I fail to come up to the challenge, my conscience will forgive me because my conscience is my Father's will, and he wills to forgive me if I fail. The Good News operates in conscience as well. For a follower of Jesus, conscience is not a tyrant but a loving invitation. "Reach for the stars: I will catch you if you fall".

Everyone by his actions reveals the God he serves. We cannot escape "the incarnation", because there is no one who does not "make flesh" the god he worships. "By their fruits you shall know them", as Jesus suggested. Worship money, and you will become like money. How we, sinners that we are, can join forces with the sinless Jesus, who always managed to do his Father's will, is by getting up each time we fall, confident in the loving concern of the One who calls us. The more often we fall and get up again, the bigger-hearted we show our God to be. How else could Jesus promise that some of us would do greater things than he himself did (John 14:12)?

●

Confirmation celebrates God's call

The christian ceremony of confirmation celebrates the call of God. Baptism celebrates the gift of God, but confirmation celebrates his call to us to be like him. In baptism God is our light and we are enlightened; God is the rock and we are securely built on his love; God is the shepherd and we are the sheep and the lambs of his flock; God is the fisherman and we are the fish in his net; God leads us and we are disciples; God is the servant or slave and we are waited upon. In confirmation we celebrate the permanent call God offers to all the baptised, to be in our turn light, rock, shepherd, fisher of men, leader, servant and slave.

The strength to respond in loving service comes from the inspiration of being called, and being called by God. We can all rise to great heights if someone sufficiently wonderful believes in us and asks for help — especially if he thinks no worse of us for failing.

●

Transfiguration

The incident in the gospels known as the transfiguration of Jesus may be thought of as the model of the christian ceremony of confirmation. The transfiguration follows the baptism of Jesus, it does not come first. Somehow it matches and balances the baptism. Whereas in the baptism the voice from heaven said "You are my beloved Son", in the transfiguration the voice says to the rest of the people present, "This is my beloved Son; listen to him". Listen to him, saying what? Listen to him as he demonstrates by word and example what God is really like; listen to the word made flesh; listen to him on trial for his life not worrying what to say, but answering up, "Yes, I am the Son of the Blessed One".

The cloud and the glory that transfigures Jesus is the glory of the Spirit, who inspires us to answer God's call and speak out the word of God with confidence.

In our confirmation ceremony we are celebrating what God says about each candidate: "This is my beloved son; listen to him", or "This is my beloved daughter, listen to her".

●

The character of confirmation

If the "character" of baptism is that it gives us each a permanent place at the table, then the "character" of confirmation is that it gives us a share in the chalice.

42

The chalice or cup is Jesus' way of speaking about his Father's will for him, and our Father's will for us. We each have our own destiny and calling. There is a song to sing that only you can sing, and another song to be sung that only I can sing. You are called to be just like your Father, and you-just-like-your-Father is something only you can ever be. I am called to be just like my Father, and me-just-like-my-Father is something only I can ever be. "To him who conquers I will give a white stone, with a name written upon it which no one knows, except him to whom it is given" (Revelation 2:17).

Once given, therefore, it never needs giving again. If we had to re-confirm failures, we would be denying God's unconditional love for the person that is confirmed, and implying that he had stopped calling because of lack of response from the disciple.

Morality is freely undertaken as a *Thank you* to God who loves us first. As the psalmist says, "How can I repay the Lord for his goodness to me? I will take the cup of salvation, I will call on God's name" (cf. Psalm 115).

●

God's will not a foregone conclusion

The wise do not think of God's will as something already fixed. There is no blueprint up in God's mind inscribed (in my case) "Gerald O'Mahony — Assembly Instructions". If I fail God at any stage he does not have to do a patching job on me so that I will fit the blueprint again. There is no blueprint for the human race, either.

God is the shepherd; I am the sheep. If I follow him, well and good. If I go astray, he comes searching after me. He does not sit sulking in the place where I ought to be. God relates to me, and calls me, exactly where I am, and no matter how I got there. God relates to the human

43

race, and calls us, exactly where we are. Like a good parent, God has no unchangeable ideas about what he wants his child to be when he grows up. If the child comes up with something unexpected and original, the good parent is delighted. If the child turns out to be a dreamer who never gets anything much done, the good parent continues to love, and hopes that real growth will come to the child out of the security of being loved regardless of results. If the child goes through a mental or moral breakdown, the good parent stands by and tries to present the very simplest of steps towards recovery.

REDEMPTION

The Cross as a sacrifice

Why is the crucifixion of Jesus spoken of as a sacrifice?
Why did the apostles think of his death and resurrection
as the sacrifice to end all sacrifices?

In the dark days before the coming of Christ, it was felt
necessary to perform ceremonies to placate the mysterious
powers of the universe, however many they might be.
Even the Jewish people, who believed in only the One God
and a loving God at that, still had sacrifices: holocausts,
communion sacrifices, atonement sacrifices, and other kinds
as well. In a holocaust the whole victim was burnt on the
altar, after the priest had sprinkled the blood of the victim
round the altar. In a communion sacrifice, after the blood
of the victim had been sprinkled round the altar, part of
the victim was given to God, by burning it on the altar, part
was given to the priest to eat, and part was taken by the
family offering the gift. In atonement sacrifices, no part of
the victim was eaten, but again its blood was sprinkled,
to cleanse the people of their sins and to mend the
covenant that had been broken.

Sacrifices cost something. To withhold the first fruits of
the harvest, the best animals in the flock or herd, or to
destroy them as a sign to God that his people recognised
all that grows as a gift from him, this cost something.
There were even times in history when a family would
sacrifice one of its own beloved children in hopes of
getting the powers, or the Power, on their side again.

After Jesus had died, and been seen again in the glory
of the resurrection, and the Spirit had dawned on the
community of his followers at Pentecost, there gradually

47

dawned also on the community the startling realisation that the sacrifices they were still regularly offering (e.g., Acts 21:26) in the temple at Jerusalem were irrelevant now. Once a man or woman can call God *"Abba! Father!"* and trust God accordingly, then there is no longer any point in going through careful rituals to get God on our side, since he is on our side already, before we start.

The event that brought the edifice of temple sacrifices tumbling down (metaphorically) and made them seem unnecessary was the death of Jesus. He had preached the Good News, but it was only in his death that the disciples saw the Good News in action, and only in the resurrection that they believed it for all time. So somewhere in that death and resurrection was the end of sacrifices.

Very soon the next logical step was taken by the apostles. Jesus' death must itself have been a sacrifice, and such a perfect sacrifice, it rendered all other sacrifices redundant, past, present and to come. He was the victim: he reminded them of the lambs and bullocks slain on the altars. His blood had been sprinkled as the new covenant was born. He was the priest: he reminded them of the high priest going through to the holy of holies, the presence of God, to intercede for men. He had been lifted up like the fragrance of incense and proved completely pleasing to God. He had offered himself, in an obedience which was better than sacrifice.

Strange things that Jesus had said came back to them, strange echoes of the Old Testament that had not always been seen as prophecies. Jesus was the Lamb of God, lambs were led to the slaughter and did not protest; Jesus was the servant, the shepherd who does not run away, but gives his life for his sheep. He was a ransom for many, for all humanity. The High Priest's words, "One man must die to save the people", took on a new significance.

Well, then, it had happened. All is well between mankind and God, once and for all, because somebody finally called him *"Abba!* Father!"" and refused to back down no matter what the cost. Christ shattered the darkness of the ages. That was all God was waiting for, hoping for, planning for, from the beginning of time.

●

The obedience of Jesus

Jesus in the garden of Gethsemani the night before he died had a choice. He could run away, or stay and face the consequences of his teaching. If he ran, there were further choices. He could run away back to Galilee, and once there either stop teaching or change his message. He could keep silent, or join with the nationalists, or the teachers of righteousness, or the Establishment, changing his message to suit theirs. If he had gone silent altogether, his enemies might have forgotten about him, and let him be. Now was Jesus' last real chance to "come down from the cross"; once he was arrested it would be too late.

But what would have been the meaning of Jesus' running away at this time? He would have been untrue to his Father, and he would have let all mankind down. To have run away at a time like that, after claiming to be telling the truth from God, would have been showing the world a God who loves us up to a certain point, but no further, a God whose love has a breaking-point. "Whoever sees me, Philip, sees the Father" was at the heart of Jesus' vocation. After saying something like that, if Jesus had run away he would have been denying that we can call God *"Abba!"*, and showing instead a God who cannot be trusted.

The question that Jesus was asked during his trial was a loaded one: "Are you the Christ, the Son of the Blessed One?" Under the circumstances, what it meant was, "Do you claim the right to call God 'Abba!' and trust him as your intimate Father? Do you claim the same right for sinners, for the sick, for foreigners, for every man and woman ever born?" To have backed down then would have been to fail in doing his Father's will. Jesus would have been disobedient, unfaithful, untrue. His Father would have forgiven him. We must believe that, just as we must believe Jesus was free to obey his inner vision or to deny it. But God could not have raised Jesus from the dead and proclaimed him right if Jesus had given a false picture of God.

Jesus was obedient even to dying for his version of what God is like.

●

Saviour

If Jesus had run away from the garden of Gethsemani, he would also have deserted you and me. There is no knowing how we would ever have dared to call God *"Abba!"* and find forgiveness for our sins, if Jesus had given a false picture of God in the hour of his trial. We know of the depths of God's mercy because the apostles had the courage to preach it; they had the courage to preach it because they had witnessed Jesus raised from the dead by the power of God alone; Jesus was raised from the dead by God's power because he was the faithful and true image of his Father.

We, along with the poor, the blind, the deaf, the lame, the lepers, the paralysed, the gentiles, the sinners, would have had our hopes raised — if indeed we ever got to hear about Jesus of Nazareth — only to have them dashed to the ground at the last minute. In this sense, we all died with Jesus, and have risen again with him. All our hope died in his death, but has risen for ever in his rising.

God is our saviour (Titus 3:4), because he is the one Lord of life and he calls us his children. Jesus is our saviour, because he is the one from whom we heard about God as Father; he is the one through whom we found the courage to believe; he is the one in whom, and under whose wing, we dare to approach God as our Father.

●

Redemption

The whole process of getting sinful humankind into a right relationship with God is called the redemption or the atonement. *Atonement* is an old English word meaning "at-one-making", the process of getting two parties at one with each other. *Redemption* is a word borrowed from the process of freeing slaves, gaining their liberty, usually by means of someone paying for their freedom. Redemption is like a ransom.

Obviously there is no question of anybody paying God for mankind's freedom. Still less is there any question of paying the devil or the forces of evil for mankind's freedom, though mankind was enslaved by evil. Freedom was obtained for all men, however, so in that sense mankind was redeemed. The redemption cost Jesus his life-blood: no question but that was the price he had to pay to stay faithful to his Father and to carry the message to you and me. When St Peter calls the blood of Christ "precious" he is thinking of how precious it was to Jesus, and how precious it was to the human race (1 Peter 1:19). The price of thirty pieces of silver was quoted and remembered because it fell so infinitely short of the real cost, and the real value, of that blood.

Did God send Jesus to his death? If we imagine God the Father saying to God the Son somewhere in eternity, "Son, the only thing that will satisfy me regarding those human beings is if you become one and die on a cross down there . . .", then the answer has to be No. God did not order his own Son's death. But if we see Jesus in the garden

51

struggling to be faithful to his conscience, then we can say that not for the first time and not for the last time a man was obedient to God's will even unto death. There are times when my life is less important than the truth I hold, and I pray to be given the power to choose the truth. The difference in Jesus' case is that the truth he died for set the whole world free.

●

Jesus emptied himself

"Jesus, though equal to God, emptied himself, taking the form of a servant or slave", says St Paul (cf. Philippians 2: 6f).The words "servant" and "slave" should alert us to expect that this process is not confined to Jesus alone. (God is servant; Jesus is servant; Peter is servant; you and I are servants.)

There is a sense in which every child is equal to its father, since both share the same nature. Jesus called God *"Abba! Father!"* but did not presume on the relationship. He knew it, he believed it, but he acted instead like a servant or a slave.

A very revealing exchange between Jesus and Peter takes place over the question of paying the half-shekel tax to the temple authorities (Matthew 17:24-27). The conclusion is, that Jesus and Peter are God's sons, so strictly speaking there is no tax to pay to God. Nevertheless, Jesus tells Peter to go fishing, and to pay tax for them both.

Heaven is free. There is no entrance fee in terms of morality. Heaven is our inheritance, not our wages. There is no question of "Be good, or God won't let you have your inheritance". Doing his Father's will was not a condition which had to be fulfilled before God would love Jesus. Following his conscience was not a condition Peter had to fulfil before God would love him. In Jesus' story of the prodigal son, the son says to himself, "I will arise and go to my father, and I will say to him, 'Father, I have sinned against heaven and before you; I am no longer worthy to be called your son; treat me as one of your hired servants' ". In the event the father does not even let the son finish his speech (Luke 15:21).

Nevertheless, Jesus gave the example of obedience. Heaven is free. "Being good", seeking our Father's will, following our conscience is the tax a loving child willingly and unnecessarily undertakes as a *Thank you* to a loving Father who will give us our inheritance tax-free, without payment.

Parents do not demand obedience and service from their children as a condition of loving the child. But they usually get it, freely given.

Morality is the imitation of God. You and I do not have to imitate him in order to earn his love. If we wish to thank him, we will want to be like him. What is God like? God is like a slave or a servant. God does not put on airs, or boast, or sit down and expect to be waited on. So we, his children, will take the hint from Jesus our brother, who performed the servant's task of washing the feet of the Twelve before their final supper together. He wanted to make sure that their last memory of him in the flesh had the priorities right (John 13:1-11).

We cannot benefit God directly, but we can show our desire to serve God by serving and forgiving those whom he has chosen as his children. His will is to love all men, not just me. The more I treat my fellow humans as princes and princesses, the higher I am prizing my own inheritance.

St Ignatius of Loyola had a way of saying, "Act as if everything depends on you; believe that everything depends on God". One might say, "Act like a slave and a servant, but believe like a prince or princess".

53

We human beings left to ourselves dream of being kings, while we are serfs. The way of Jesus is exactly the reverse: as disciples of Jesus, we dream of being serfs, while we are kings.

●

The drop of water

"By the mixing of this water and wine, may we come to share in the divinity of Christ, who humbled himself to share in our humanity." The drop of water used in the preparation of the gifts at the Eucharist contains the mystery of the Son who acts as a slave.

Wine symbolises the divine. Water, like bread, here symbolises all that is simply human. Although Jesus was the divine Son (wine), he took on our slavery (water), so that we slaves could become free of tax, divine sons and daughters like himself. Jesus is turning the water which is us into the wine which is himself.

●

Grace

What kind of reality is "grace"? I am sure the word was taught to me too young, because I as a child immediately tried to put a picture to it and make it a "thing". It was, in my imagination, a supernatural thing like milk: like liquid because God could pour it into people, white because it made my soul white, a thing because God could give people more or less of it, supernatural because that was what the catechism said.

The catechism never actually said what grace is. The definition evaded the issue. If a child asks his parents, "What are you giving me for Christmas?", and they answer,

"A gift", the child knows he has to wait till December 25 to unwrap the gift and find out what it is. So to tell me as the catechism did that grace is a supernatural gift of God freely bestowed on me for my sanctification and salvation actually told me nothing. I still asked myself, "What is grace?"

Eventually a wise guide told me, that grace is a relationship. Grace is the same kind of reality that relationships are. Grace is like having a wife or a husband, a friend, a father, a mother, a brother, a sister. Grace works like that. Having a friend can change a person. Having a wife or a husband one did not have before can change a person.

God's grace, then, is being able to call God *"Abba! Father!"* There is the free gift, when we unwrap it. Not only that, but grace is having Jesus for my brother, and the Spirit for my spirit, living in me and taking me over.

Grace comes to us with baptism, or whenever a person learns to call God *"Abba! Father!"* or learns to trust that the deepest reality is incurably friendly. There are numerous breakthroughs as the relationship starts and grows. His love for me is always there. My eyes are only opened gradually, and the relationship is built up by degrees. For a christian, the relationship is expressed perfectly from the start in the ceremony of baptism, but the actual dawning may come before, during and long after the celebration.

"Abba! Father!" cannot be spoken without a father, a child, and a spirit. Jesus was the first to say it to God as his Father, in their own Spirit. We say it now by the gift of God.

●

Like little children

Time and again Jesus tells us to be like little children. A little child calls its father *"Abba!"* Jesus wants us to be like that in regard to God. The best way into the mystery of God is to call him *"Abba! Father!"* and trust him as a child trusts in its parents' love.

"God loves me unconditionally, not because I am good but because I am his". Once I believe that, and rely upon it at all times as my one and only security, then I have become like a little child.

●

Conversion; repentance

Becoming like a little child, and being converted, and believing the Good News, are all one and the same. Repentance and conversion are one and the same. Any person who is afraid of God needs to undergo a change of heart before he can believe God loves him without strings attached.

●

Amendment

Mending my ways, being good from now onwards, comes as a result of being forgiven. It is not a condition of being forgiven. God loves me even in the midst of my sins. Once I see that, as St Paul saw it and so many others have seen it, *then* I am sorry, *then* I do not want to displease him again, *then* I want to be like him, *then* I want to forgive others as I have been forgiven.

Jesus told Simon the Pharisee to look at the woman who wept tears over his feet and wiped them with her hair, and who anointed and kissed his feet. She loved Jesus because all her sins were forgiven, not the other way round (cf. Luke 7:36-50). She did not have her sins forgiven because she loved so much, but she loved so much because she found her sins forgiven.

Jesus went to have a meal at Zacchaeus' house before, not after, Zacchaeus decided to mend his ways (Luke 19:1-10).

●

Faith

Faith is believing that I can call God *"Abba!"* Faith is trusting in him as a child trusts an ever-loving parent. Faith is believing that therefore my sins are forgiven. Faith is picking up and putting on the white garment. Faith is accepting God's offer and rejoicing to be his child.

In that sense, faith does justify me. God says I am his child, if I will only believe him. Good works, good deeds, morality, that comes afterwards, as summer and autumn follow the spring, as my *Thank you* to the God whose mercy I have believed in.

My faith is based on Jesus. I believe I can call God "Father!" because of the life, death and resurrection of Jesus Christ my Lord.

The faith that justifies me is the same power that makes my enemies my brothers. I had better take my foot off the neck of any other child of God I find myself standing on. God is that child's Father, too.

God forgives us if we forgive one another. God is my Father and our Father. I believe and we believe.

●

Fear of God

"The fear of the Lord" which is the beginning of wisdom is not the same thing as being afraid of God. To be scared of God is the very opposite of believing the Good News, and is moreover the oldest of all sins and the origin of all sins. "The fear of the Lord" which is praised in scripture means being afraid to seek my security anywhere else but in Yahweh, who turns out to be the Father of Jesus.

Fear of the Lord means building one's life on the rock which is Jesus' word: "You can call God 'Abba! Father!' "

Building a great tower of good deeds so as to enter heaven without any need for God to stoop down is not good fear of the Lord. Nor is digging a hole in the ground and burying your talent.

The lost sheep is not afraid of the shepherd; he is afraid of anyone else. A lost child is not afraid of the sight of his parents; he is afraid of anyone else. The builder is not afraid of the rock. He is afraid of the sand.

●

The seed

In the parables told by Jesus, the seed that is sown, germinates and grows is the seed of faith in the word of God. The word of God is, "You are my beloved child; with you I am well pleased". When that word takes root in my mind and heart, then the seed has started growing.

That seed starts as a tiny event, but grows until it fills the whole of a person's consciousness and every corner of every day, and eventually other people come to find security and shade (as birds come to roost in a shrub, as sheep come to a shepherd, as builders come to a rock, as mariners take directions from a light). What starts as faith, grows into love. What starts as trust, grows into good works. What starts as a sheep, turns into a shepherd. What starts as a seed, turns into a seed-bearer. What starts as a baptised christian becomes a confirmed christian.

The seed grows of its own accord. God speaks the word in the first place, and he does not waste his words. He chose us, we did not first choose him.

●

Prayer

Prayer is the language between mankind and God. It follows the various strands of our relationship with God and expresses them. For a follower of Jesus, Jesus' own prayer and the way he taught us to pray become the models. The way we pray is the way we believe, and Jesus nowhere more clearly expresses the news he came to bring us than in the way he prays and teaches us to pray.

In the garden, the night before he died, Jesus prayed, "*Abba!* Father! all things are possible to you; remove this cup from me; yet not what I want, only what you want". He taught his disciples to pray, "Our Father . . . "

Prayer, then, is calling God "*Abba!*", and is the language of faith. Prayer means gratitude, being clothed in the white garment of the risen Christ, asking forgiveness. Prayer is the language of those who receive the gift of God. Prayer is also the word that goes with wanting to show gratitude to God by becoming like God. "Thy will be done, not mine". Prayer is searching for the will of God, and asking for the strength to be like him. Prayer is starting to do the things we know God wants, trusting that the power will be given to us.

Wherever the relationship which we have called "grace" goes, there prayer goes. We pray in the Spirit, with Jesus, to the Father. We can pray to Jesus at the right hand of

God. We can ask the Spirit to be our Counsel and Advocate, and to dwell in us and to speak in us.

We disciples of Jesus can ask one another for help, and thank one another, and seek the best ways to help one another, because God helps us through other disciples, and other disciples through us, when we imitate Jesus and love one another with his Spirit.

The most precious gift to be found in prayer is hope. God can at times remove the clouds and reveal the reality of Jesus and his love for us. Deep down, that is what every christian seeks in prayer, to see Jesus at the right hand of God. God can give proofs of his love, which give the traveller heart to persevere to the end.

●

No strange gods

Whatever god we worship, we become like that god. Those who worship money become more and more like money. Those who worship success become more and more like success, praising and condemning by the rules of success, damning themselves if they fail.

Each of us is a temple. Each of us has a Holy of Holies, with a god enthroned. Disciples of Jesus seek to enthrone there no god but the God and Father of Jesus, the God who forgives, the God we can call *"Abba!"*

Those who enthrone any other god quickly find themselves "reaping the whirlwind", crushed by the weight of the burden their false god imposes on them.

Every form of idolatry has its own "grace", its own relationship, its own forms of prayer. You can guess at what kind of god people worship, by listening to their prayers.

●

60

Love

"Faith is the beginning, the end is love", wrote St Ignatius of Antioch. The love that matters is God's love for us, first, then our love in return.

Jesus sent his disciples out in twos. The witness of two people united in love is a brighter light than the witness of one person talking about love.

Jesus taught us to pray "Our Father", not simply "My Father", because everyone is God's favourite. St Peter and St Paul both tell us that God has no favourites (cf. Acts 10:34; Romans 2:11), but another way of saying the same truth is to say that everyone is God's favourite. I am God's favourite, and so are you.

When the Jewish people saw themselves as the Chosen People, they were seeing something true about themselves. They are God's chosen people. But the inspiration did not yet go deep enough. Every people is God's favourite people; the Jews were simply the first to hear what God is saying.

There is one major difference between the Jewish concept of "the people of God" and the christian "kingdom of God" or "people of God". As seen through christian eyes, the salvation God offered to the Jews was to the Jewish people. The people were more important than the individual. If the individual deserted the people, he was lost. Whereas in the christian "kingdom of God" one does not have to qualify by coming up to any standard of behaviour or good fortune of birth. Any blind, lame, leprous, or paralysed person, any man or woman of any colour or race, good, bad or indifferent as regards moral behaviour *is* a child of God and a favourite of God. There is never any question of sacrificing the individual for the good of the whole people. Like any good family, the human race must take its time by the slowest among us. If we leave even the least little one behind, we leave Christ behind. Surely, no favourite could ask for better conditions than those.

THE CHURCH AND SACRAMENTS

Church

The church is the community of the resurrection, that is, the community of those who believe, on account of the life, death and resurrection of Jesus, that it is safe to call God *"Abba!"* The select band of people who saw and heard Jesus in his public ministry and followed him, who then witnessed his death and burial, and finally his resurrection, were already a community of sorts before his death.

After his resurrection and the coming of the Spirit at Pentecost, the witnesses could not escape the sense of "mission", of vocation. Here were they now, the ones who knew as deeply as Jesus could have wished that his truth was from God, and that therefore mankind can call God *"Abba!* Father!" They knew, and they alone in the world knew, so the only possible course of action was to tell the world.

In so many ways, Jesus had built them up as a community in order that their light would shine brighter. The heart of the community lay in the fact that they all knew, in the Spirit, how to call God *"Abba!* Father!" as Jesus had taught them. Next, as a community they wanted to thank God by imitating him, so that people would look at them and say, "Now I see the God you are speaking of". Thus the disciples would become the light of the world; thus they would become a sign, a sacrament, to show to all men the God men cannot see. "All men" includes men and women of today and every day. Thus we, the present-day disciples, are now the church.

From the start there were disputes about the right way and the wrong way of proceeding, and about matters great and small. Disputes have been there ever since. However, the church, the gathering of Jesus' followers can still be a lighthouse, so long as the God enthroned in the community's temple is the God of forgiveness.

"We believe in the forgiveness of sins" is actually easier, not harder, to demonstrate where sin is to be found.

●

Right hand, left hand

(In all courtesy it should be pointed out that readers who are left-handed will have to read "left" for "right" and vice versa, in this section. Readers who are ambidextrous will have to be patient with the rest of us.)

We can easily take fright for the wrong reasons at some of Jesus' parables, as if they were dividing mankind into good people and bad people, whereas they are dividing the good from the bad in people. The physical trait he often uses as an illustration of the spiritual truth is right-handedness. With our right hand we can do all sorts of things well, that we can only bungle with our left hand.

When Jesus tells his parable of the Son of Man "separating them one from another as a shepherd separates the sheep from the goats" we can, if we are honest, recognise ourselves on both sides of the dividing line. "I was hungry and you fed me", says the king. Every mother in her kitchen, every man who has cooked for others, every wage-earner who has brought home the family's daily bread, they can all recognise themselves among the sheep. "I was hungry and you gave me no food", says the king. And everyone who has ever passed over an appeal for the starving can recognise himself among the goats.

For every sick person or prisoner we have visited, there are a greater number we have not visited. The sheep go on the right hand, the goats on the left. Some actions I get right, other actions are foreign to me even while I do them. I am both sheep and goat.

Think of the parable of the ten bridesmaids, and count them on your own fingers. Five are ready and waiting (on the right hand); five are sluggish and unresponsive (on the left hand).

Think of the parable of the weeds sown in the corn. There is more profit in the story if we think of the field as "me", "this human being", than if we think of it as "the human race". If we think it means "the human race" we are tempted to picture some human beings as shoots of corn and some as weeds. We are inclined to appoint ourselves as judges, and either write people off or fail to see any evil in them. Whereas if the field is "me", then in me there is corn, and in me there are weeds. In me there is a moral and spiritual "right hand" and "left hand".

The "right hand" is imperishable, like God. The "left-hand" is perishable, like Adam and Eve. Think of the "good thief" crucified on the right hand side of Jesus, and the "bad thief" crucified on his left. St Luke tells of the fact, but makes a parable of it at the same time.

The way the whole person is saved, and comes to stand with Jesus at the right side of God, "clothed in white garments, on the right side" like the young men in the resurrection accounts, is through love and forgiveness. The more a person becomes aware of God's love and forgiveness, the more he will perform "right handed" actions, which have eternal value.

The church, and indeed the world, is made up of people who are a mixture of good and bad, each of us containing in ourselves both sheep and goat, wise and foolish bridesmaids, corn and weeds, good thief and bad thief. The time of judgement is not yet. God is always, like a loving Father, hoping that the tree will maybe bear fruit this season, giving time for the good in us to conquer the evil, for the right hand to forgive the left hand so that we end up in total peace.

●

Judgement

Jesus did not come to judge the world but to save the world (John 12:47).

There are two conditions attached to salvation. They are "built-in", and there is no way even God can bypass them, since they are in the nature of reality. Both are gifts of God, and will be given to us as we ask for them.

The first is the power to believe that God is my *Abba*, my intimate Father.

The second is the willingness to forgive everyone else whom God has forgiven. "Judge not", said Jesus, "and you will not be judged" (Luke 6:37).

To those who turn to him in trust, God is the rock of salvation. Upon those who do not trust, the rock of their own false gods will fall. For those who call God *"Abba!"*, their sufferings will be a purifying fire; for those who trust in any other god, the fire will be hostile, because the things they have trusted in are perishable.

There is only one pure gold, which cannot be destroyed by fire, only one precious stone which is imperishable: God's love for us as his children. No point in setting my heart on riches, since God loves me whether I am rich or poor; no point in worshipping honour or glory or fame or good looks or talent or health, since God loves me whether I am disgraced or honoured, obscure or famous, ugly or beautiful, dull or talented, sick or well.

Even to pride myself on my good deeds is to create a false god. I might feed the hungry, give drink to the thirsty, welcome the stranger, clothe the naked, visit the sick and the imprisoned all the hours God gives me, but if I thought that my actions earned me heaven and gave me a right to condemn those whose actions were evil, I would be in for a rude shock . . . like the labourers in the vineyard, or the elder brother of the prodigal son, in Jesus' stories.

For every one person I help, there are a hundred I never helped, so I cannot safely stake my claim to salvation on how many people I helped. Even if a generation should one day arrive when all the world's social problems are solved, the solutions will have been found by the gift of God.

The essential ingredient of every good act is that it should be a *Thank you* to God who even gives us the very power to say *Thank you*. For this reason it is better not to let my left hand know what my right hand is doing, when I give alms or do anything good.

●

Death

Death is, for each one of us, the time when everything perishable perishes. Rust is forming and leaves are falling all the time, and the evidence is always in front of our eyes. Fear of death is perfectly natural for any member of the animal kingdom, and is an essential factor in survival and self-preservation. Human beings have an added inclination to fear death, since death is seen as the time of judgement.

Jesus tells me that the everlasting God loves me as his child. God loves me whether I am dark or fair, young or old . . . alive or dead. The covenant formed by Jesus between God and me cannot be broken even by death. Jesus seems to have implied as much before his own death (e.g., Mark

12:27; John 11:25), and the resurrection of Jesus made it clear to the witnesses.

Jesus shows me how best to die. Humans nearly always like to round off what they are doing, to end with a flourish no matter what they have been engaged in. Few have the energy or the concentration to die with a flourish. Jesus died, so the gospels tell us, insisting that he was right in calling God *"Abba!* Father!", and forgiving his enemies. He gave up his life as a *Thank you,* back into his Father's hands from whom he had received it: "Father, into your hands I commit my life".

There was precious little evidence for Jesus to go on. To many of the onlookers it was obvious that if Jesus really was right to call God "Father!", God would not have left him to die on a cross. Jesus himself may well have felt completely abandoned (cf. Mark 15:34).

The statement of the Apostles' Creed, that Jesus Christ "descended into hell", is saying that Jesus really died and was buried, joining all those before him in the human race who had died and been buried. In embracing the leper he had taken God's love to the outcast. His burial includes all those who died before him in the "all men" for whom he lived, died, and rose again. The new translation of the Apostles' Creed included in our missals since 1966 actually says "He descended to the dead" in place of "He descended into hell".

●

Hell

Hell is the state of those (if any there be) who have refused to accept God as Father, or to share God's forgiveness with the others whom God has forgiven.

Christian churches have never said that any dead person is in hell . . . not Judas, not Hitler, not anybody. All they

70

teach is that life is a deadly serious business, because hell is a real possibility, and our one lifetime is the limit of time available to us to accept or refuse God's love. In secular terms, a person in real danger would be one who will not be loved or love anyone, will not accept forgiveness or forgive anyone.

God does not send anyone to hell, so anyone who trusts in God need not fear hell from God. It is not in God's power to send anyone to hell. Remember, fear of God is the original sin and the origin of all other sins: Jesus' whole life and mission was dedicated to ridding us of that needless fear. We are in hell already until Jesus comes to rescue us by providing the ladder to God: *"Abba! Father!"*

●

Purgatory

Purgatory is the name given to the state of those who are being purified (like gold in the furnace) on the way to God. The name can apply both to those of us who have not yet died, and to those who have died. The process of learning to trust God as the only everlasting value is a painful one to human beings, composed as we are of perishable and imperishable dreams. It is hard to accept that riches and physical beauty and music and friendship and sexual love and physical strength and a thousand other wonders of life are doomed to die on the day I die; it is painful to lose them all one by one as I grow older, and to realise little by little that God loves me with or without them. In the end, nothing else matters but his love for me as his child.

Catholics have always prayed either *to* their dead brothers and sisters or *for* them. Each Catholic community has an instinct for deciding which is more appropriate in each case.

When we pray for the dead we are praying that God who is all mercy will have mercy on those for whom we pray; we are thanking God for all the gifts he gave us through their lives; and we are praying that the good they did may live on in us, but that any evil they did may either be turned to good or be forgotten and not live on.

●

Saints

Prayer is not always a conversation conducted across the fence of death. When I ask a brother or sister to help me, I am praying. When they help me, they are praying.

Those christians who refuse to pray to saints who have died seem to me to be inconsistent. I can ask Ignatius of Loyola or Vincent de Paul to help me when they are alive, without taking away from the saving power of Christ; so why cannot I continue to ask them when they die? Of course I can carry on praying to them.

They help me after death chiefly through the example, the inspiration and the memory they leave behind, which can be illuminated in my mind and heart by God. And if I can talk to my Father about them, why should they not talk to him about me?

●

Heaven

Heaven is the enjoyment of God as my Father. Like judgement, hell and purgatory, heaven is not limited to after death. After death, however, we believe it will be unmixed with sorrow, unmixed with what perishes.

The images for heaven in scripture and other literature are numberless: banquet, victory, city of jewels, perpetual sunshine and spring, harvest, homecoming, rescue, top of the ladder, triumph, green pasture for the sheep, safe harbour for the boat, waking from sleep, sleep and rest after labour, reward, wages, holiday, splendid robes, shining like stars, palaces, inheritance, treasure, sight, hearing, recovery, healing . . .

I possess it now really and truly, but in hope, through Jesus my anchor.

Since God is unfathomable, we need not think of heaven as static. It may turn out to be more like a process, as we explore the depth and the height and the breadth of God's love for us as his children.

●

Sacrament

Jesus is the sacrament of God. A sacrament is a sign that makes visible the invisible God, so Jesus is a sacrament. Jesus is *the* sacrament, because as the one and only Son of God he makes God visible in a way no one else could. It is because Jesus makes God visible in a way no one else could, and gives us a perfect and living picture of God, that we call him the true and only Son of God.

The church of Jesus' disciples is a sacrament also. You and I, disciples of Christ, are sacraments, because our vocation is to make people who look at us say, "Ah, now I see what God is like". We together can be a living and visible sign of the God that we can see (through Christ), but that the world cannot see.

●

The Church's Seven Sacraments

There are seven special celebrations within the community of the resurrection. Rather as white light can be split by a

73

prism into the seven colours of the rainbow (red, orange, yellow, green, blue, indigo, violet), so the one light of Christ can be seen under seven aspects. No one celebration, no one symbol (apart from the whole life and death of Jesus of Nazareth) can fully express his light, but the seven celebrations we call the seven sacraments between them keep the church focussed upon the main message and impact of Jesus Christ.

Water can express new life, perils gone through, enemies drowned, but bread is a better symbol of feeding the traveller; anointing can express healing, or royal election, but marriage vows exchanged are a better expression of everlasting love.

Baptism, Confirmation, the Eucharist, Penance, Anointing of the Sick, Ordination and Marriage are all called Sacraments, because they are visible signs of the God we cannot see, who was revealed to us in Jesus Christ. Jesus himself comes across to us in words and actions; the seven sacraments all have actions whose meaning is made clear in words, always including the words of Jesus himself.

Baptism we have already considered at some length. The reader may like to recall the sections dealing with baptism, light, water, candle, original sin and adoption, and indeed all the early pages of this book. We have also considered the sacrament of confirmation to some extent. In addition, we may think now of those ceremonies as a visible sign of the invisible God who was revealed in Jesus.

•

Celebrations

Sacraments are signs that bring about the grace they signify. They are celebrations that bring about the very reality that they celebrate. The celebration of a sacrament cannot be taken in isolation from our understanding of the

74

symbols used. The celebration of a sacrament cannot either be taken in isolation from our experience, in the life of our christian community, of what the sacraments symbolise. Symbols are by their nature hazy round the edges, luminous, not so clear-cut in meaning as definitions. Happily, no description can fully pin symbols down.

Baptism, then, celebrates the gift of God. It is celebrating entry into the community where nobody will judge the new candidate, but everyone will adopt him as a fellow child of God and a fellow guest at the banquet. But baptism also creates the community and its christian attitudes.

Where in baptism God says, "You are my beloved child; with you I am well pleased", in *confirmation* he says to the assembly: "This is my beloved child: listen to him (listen to her)". After the time of being loved, comes the time of loving in return, the time of service, of witness, of incarnation. God provides the power, by the inspiration of his call and through the example and company of the adult community. Confirmation celebrates the call of God, but also creates the framework in which God's call is heard in the church.

In the *Eucharist,* we celebrate (to mention but one aspect) the presence of Christ in word and sacrament. But we are all the more aware of the reality of his presence as our food for the journey if the scriptures which are read make sense because we daily see them put into action. We pray that when we receive the body and blood of Christ we may become one body, one spirit in Christ. The more this unity becomes a reality in our daily lives, the more we are aware of the reality of his presence.

The sacrament of *penance* (or reconciliation) celebrates the forgiveness Jesus brings: not the initial covenant, "I will be your Father", which we celebrate in baptism, but the way this same covenant does not break under repeated shocks from us. It brings about an atmosphere of forgiveness in the community, and benefits from an atmosphere of forgiveness in the community.

Anointing the sick and praying over them reminds the community of Jesus' care for the sick, and brings about a more dedicated and hopeful style of nursing; the warmth and prayerful care of the community in its turn makes the symbol of anointing more effective for the patient.

Jesus promised to be with his church to the end of time, and to the ends of the earth. The ceremony of *ordination* celebrates the continuity of Jesus' presence from one generation to the next, and from one place to the next. The greater the links with past and future, and with other dioceses and christian groups near and far, the more the ceremony will mean.

As the prophet Hosea foreshadowed, the bond of *marriage* is one of the greatest sacraments of the new covenant. Hosea loved an unfaithful wife, and in doing so learnt how God loves unfaithful mankind. The presence of marriages that last till death helps fickle human beings to believe that the God we cannot see will love us for better or for worse, for richer or for poorer, in sickness and health, as long as he lives. They are also a constant reminder of the way Jesus loved the church of his disciples "even unto death".

Sacraments bring about what they symbolise, and symbolise what they bring about. They celebrate aspects of the love God shows us in Christ, a love which is already "there" and real. The celebrations release the love into our lives. They celebrate a relationship; but they also create and strengthen the relationship. They celebrate grace, and give grace.

●

How sacraments work

Sacraments work in the way celebrations work. For a celebration, there has to be something to celebrate, and something to celebrate with, and someone to celebrate with.

Suppose it is George's birthday, but George is in prison, in solitary confinement with all privileges stopped. No presents, no cards, no "Happy birthday, George!" from anybody. Hardly a birthday at all. Compare George's birthday the next year, with George free and dozens of cards, hundreds of greetings, a party in the evening with presents and plenty to eat and drink, and the company of loved ones. A birthday to remember. In each case it was a real birthday, but the birthday celebrated means much more.

Similarly, the celebration of sacraments is the celebration of something which is already true . . . but the celebration brings the truth home to us. A birthday is not enormously significant; it celebrates the sun's being back in the same part of the sky as when we were born. The truths that the church's seven sacraments celebrate are vastly more significant and precious.

Every human child born is a child of God already. Jesus taught us so, and we, his disciples, celebrate the fact in baptism.

Once this relationship has been established and celebrated, the other aspects of the same adoptive love can then be celebrated at appropriate times.

God through conscience invites every human being to respond by being like himself, to love him back. Christians are the ones who celebrate the fact of this permanent "call" in confirmation. The call is for us who know Jesus a call to discipleship.

To take again just one aspect of the Eucharist, namely feeding, God is in fact feeding the minds and bodies of all mankind all the time. This is one of the things we are celebrating in the Eucharist. For christians, the feeding of us by God takes place through Jesus Christ in word and sacrament. Jesus is feeding us all the time through his

77

words working in our minds, through his sacrifice ever present in the world, and through the help we get from each other as members of his body, the church. Yet when we celebrate being fed by Jesus, the difference the celebration makes is so startling we speak of the "real presence" of Jesus in this sacrament. Indeed if we stopped celebrating the Eucharist, the community would die for lack of nourishment.

God has forgiven our sins long before we "go to confession". In confessing our sins privately and hearing the words of the gospel and the words of absolution we are celebrating something which was already true. The celebration brings the truth home to us, framed in the words and actions of Jesus. Communal penance services are celebrations of the community's forgiveness of one another in accordance with the teaching of Jesus. The communal service helps to sensitize consciences and to bring about what it celebrates.

The sacrament of anointing celebrates the care of God for the sick. God's care for the sick is to be found in every man's conscience. His care is found incarnate wherever there is compassion in the world. His care for the sick as shown to us by Jesus is already at work in christian communities, even before we celebrate it.

God already loves the human race always and everywhere, through all time and to the ends of the earth. His word has come down in Jesus, and will grow and be fruitful without our human efforts being necessary. This we celebrate in the sacrament of orders.

The marriage ceremony must have love there to celebrate, and yet it brings about the very love it is celebrating. The couple look back on the day, and the memories, and the ring, and the photographs, and the promises, and they try to live up to that day until death parts them. And all the time they are celebrating something that already exists, namely God's everlasting love for each individual person.

●

Seven aspects of the one love

Through these seven signs within the church we can see the light of Jesus as our brother, our leader, our companion, freeing us from sin, caring over the sick, with us always and everywhere, loving us personally as long as he lives "for better or for worse".

Through these seven signs we meet Jesus bringing us the adoption, call, company and forgiveness of our *Abba*, in sickness, always and everywhere, "for better or for worse". They are signs of God's love shown to us in Jesus.

They are sacraments of the new covenant between mankind and an *Abba* who is eternal, imperishable, divine.

●

Sacramental sacrifice

One of the sacraments is traditionally thought of as a sacrifice as well as a sacrament: the Eucharist. The early christian church gradually stopped attending the temple worship and sacrifices as they found they no longer needed them, but they continued to do each week what Jesus had done with the Twelve at the last supper they had together.

For christians, sacrifices stopped with the death of Jesus. His death was seen as the perfect sacrifice for all time, of which the victim was acceptable to God, lifted up like incense into the presence of God. Jesus called God "*Abba!*" and got away with it because it was true . . . because it *is* true. He taught us to do the same. There is no further need of sacrifice.

The Mass, or the Eucharist, is not and cannot be another sacrifice. It can only be the same sacrifice, presented in a sacramental way as Jesus instructed. "My body here, my blood there. Then you will always be remembering my death".

In the Passover, when the children of Israel were led by Moses, under the providence of God, to escape from Egypt through the waters, God's love shone clear. Ever afterwards, in re-enacting that night, Jewish families remind themselves, "God never changes; God loved us then; so God loves us now".

Jesus was saying at the last supper, "Do not do this in memory of Moses any more. Do it in memory of me. God's love will never be clearer to men than it is on this night. So do always as I am doing, and remember that if God loves you this much tonight, God never changes, and the love you see tonight is true till I come again and fetch you".

The Eucharist is thought of by christians as celebrating the "paschal mystery" by which we are liberated from slavery to sin through the "exodus" of Christ's passion, death and resurrection.

In the Eucharist we have, not a birthday celebrated, but a living sacrifice celebrated. The fact that we are invited to eat and drink the sacrament speaks volumes about our incorporation into everything that Jesus is and everything he does. In taking his body as our bread, we are accepting the gift of God; in taking the chalice we are answering the call of God.

●

Mediator

Jesus is the one and only mediator between God and mankind. The one and only approach to God is to call him *"Abba!* Father!" and trust him, and it was Jesus who lived and died to teach us so. Jesus was conscious that he had a mission and a vocation to teach men what he knew about the approach to God, a mission he expressed by saying God sent him to give the Good News. The resurrection showed the witnesses that God did indeed send Jesus, since now God sealed the message with an unmistakable signature. The ascension expresses the sureness of the witnesses that Jesus is now at God's right hand, as Joseph the patriarch finished up at Pharaoh's right hand.

Now, if we want anything from God we go through Jesus, using the approach and the appeal that Jesus taught us, calling God "*Abba!* Father!" Now, if God wants to tell us anything he tells us through Jesus, illuminating his words and his sacraments so that we can see our Father in Jesus.

Jesus is God incarnate, the Word of God made flesh for us to see. Jesus incorporates us with himself, and takes us to the Father who sent him. Jesus is our "Jacob's ladder", let down from heaven to earth so we could climb from earth to heaven, even as far as the Holy of Holies, the presence of God. Jesus is like a mother hen under whose wings we shelter, so that the onlooker can only see Jesus (Matthew 23:37; Luke 13:34). God looks upon us, but hears and sees his child.

Jesus is mediator of the new covenant, by which God says, "I will be your *Abba;* you will be my child". Jesus' blood was the precious blood that sprinkled the new covenant, not the blood of animals like that which Moses used to seal the old covenant.

●

The Day of the Lord

"The Day of the Lord" is an expression that keeps appearing among the writings of the Old Testament prophets. The day would come when the truth would prevail, when all that was written in the books would be revealed (Daniel 7:10), the day when the sons of Abraham would triumph. "The books" meant the diary of what actually happened in history, not the doctored history left in earthly books by the rich and powerful. As the belief of the Jewish people in an after-life began to grow, in the two or three centuries prior to the coming of Jesus, the Day of the Lord began to mean the day of resurrection, when all who had died unrevenged and unjustly dishonoured would be raised and rewarded, to the shame and confusion of their oppressors.

When Jesus was first seen raised from the dead, it was the first day of the week (e.g., John 20:1). Among the many facets of the resurrection which startled and amazed and profoundly changed the witnesses was the realisation that the Day of the Lord had arrived, even though only one person was so far raised. Jesus was unjustly condemned, and here was God vindicating him, to the confusion of his enemies. Moreover, Jesus had promised to incorporate all God's poor in his own victory, so Jesus was only the start, the first fruits of a great harvest.

The Day of the Lord had dawned. In pagan cultures, the first day of the week is often the day of the sun. The gospel records seem to have caught the symbolism of the sun risen (Mark 16:2), the light of Christ risen, the dawn of the Day of the Lord and combined them into one. Ever since then Sunday has been "the Lord's Day" for christians.

For Israelites, life is balanced where the sabbath is balanced. God has worked six days, creating; now he is resting, and his people wait for the dawning of the Day. For christians, the balance is at Sunday. The Day has arrived, and the light has already dawned which will never again be put out.

From even before the New Testament writings were complete, the christian "passover" of the Eucharist was celebrated in association with the dark of Saturday night and the dawn of Sunday morning (cf. Acts 20:7; 1 Corinthians 16:2; Hebrews 10:25). And even in those early days, there were already some christians who failed to turn up, to the disappointment and chagrin of those who were faithful (Hebrews 10:25).

THE CHURCH AND MORALITY

Conscience and the Church

I, and nobody else, can hear God calling me. Others can hear God calling them, but they cannot hear God calling me. Once I know God as my Father, I hear my Father calling me. Just as Jesus' conscience was the way to his Father's will, so my conscience is for me the way to my Father's will. "Call no man your father on earth, for you have one Father, who is in heaven", said Jesus (Matthew 23:9). Do not call your father your father, the government your father, the bishop your father, the Pope your father, your "spiritual father" your father, if what they tell you conflicts with what your Father in heaven tells you he wants. He is your Father, not they.

The *Catechism of Christian Doctrine* taught that we must obey lawful superiors "in all that is not sin". The catechism also implied, however, that the advice and moral teaching of the church and in particular the Pope could never be wrong for me, so that if I found my conscience and what the Pope said did not agree, then I was bound to obey the Pope, since he would never command what was sinful. There is a fatal flaw hidden in the implied argument, since at that rate my conscience would be bound by the conscience of another man — which is a form of moral slavery or suicide.

Traditional catholic teaching, on the contrary, has always held that I must follow my own conscience even if my own conscience is in error, so that even if we suppose the particular teaching of the Pope or other spiritual leader which conflicts with my honest judgement to be correct, I am still bound to follow my own vision, not anyone else's. In the last resort, no one else can tell me what I

85

think I ought to do. Others can only tell me what they think I ought to do. If I am sure in my heart of hearts that what others are advising or telling me to do is wrong, then no matter what spiritual or temporal authority they threaten me with I should do what I see as the truth, not what they see; I am called by God to do what I see as the truth, not what they see.

Tied up with this whole question is the notion (common but unsound) that the church has access to knowledge about right and wrong which no other people have. In fact, "revelation" (taken narrowly as meaning laws from scripture or tradition) does not supply the exact knowledge of what to do and what to avoid. That kind of "revelation" only reinforces ideas of right and wrong which we get from other ordinary (but none the less God-given) sources: experience; discussion; reasoning; study of the consequences of past actions; ethical laws and principles; interior knowledge of my own strength and weakness; listening to advice; listening to others' experience . . . and so on.

The usual way in which this basic human freedom of conscience is exercised by the mentally retarded and by children rests in their freedom of choice as to whose advice they will take. They have an instinct regarding who is trustworthy and who is not: they judge the tree by its fruits.

●

The Ten Commandments

The Ten Commandments were not ten brand new rules which dropped from heaven to Moses. They mostly existed already as ethical rules in the neighbouring cultures; they were very limited in perfection ("Thou shalt not kill" referring to members of the same race; "thou shalt not commit adultery" making no mention of fornication or any

86

other sexual sin); our christian practice of lumping all the sins we have discovered under one or other of the Ten Commandments is very interesting, but goes far beyond the Ten Commandments themselves. The inspiration of Moses was to pick out, from the existing legislation of the time, the ten rules which made all the difference between a nation and no nation, and to put them in the framework of a covenant between God and his people. He was also original in putting religious and moral laws under the same code and on the same footing. Early cultures tended to want to separate religion and morals in the same way and for the same reasons as many people today want to separate religion and politics. Moses' law insisted that if you love God you must do the right thing by other people as well.

The ten things forbidden by the Ten Commandments are "forbidden by God because they are wrong", not "wrong because forbidden by God".

●

The moral teachings of Christ

(i) The two great commandments

Jesus reduced the Ten Commandments and the whole Law of Moses to two commands: "The first is, 'Hear, O Israel: The Lord our God, the Lord is one; and you shall love the Lord your God with all your heart, and with all your soul, and with all your mind, and with all your strength.' The second is this, 'You shall love your neighbour as yourself.' There is no other commandment greater than these" (Mark 12:29-31).

The first may be thought of as corresponding to the first three of the Ten Commandments; the second may be thought of as corresponding to the remaining seven commandments (or from "Honour thy father and thy mother" to the end).

Jesus clearly presumed that a serious-minded Jew would know the Ten Commandments, and would try to keep them (Mark 10:17).

●

The moral teachings of Christ

(ii) Jesus' own commandment

Jesus gave a new commandment, "that you love one another as I have loved you" (John 13:34; 15:12). "God is *Abba*, your Father. He loves you without conditions. I have loved you unconditionally, and will do so to the end, so that you will see in me what your Father is like. Then, when you have seen what he is like, thank him by imitating him, on my pattern".

Jesus has many moral commands: "Judge not"; "Do not worry about tomorrow"; "Do not swear at all"; "When you have a party, invite those who cannot invite you back"; "Do not look dismal when you fast"; "Pray like this . . ."; "Do not lay up for yourselves treasures on earth" . . . these, and many more. They are nearly all ethical teachings which can be found in non-christian sources before as well as after the time of Jesus. Jesus adopted as his own, for instance, the Golden Rule of ethics which is much older than his day, "Do unto others as you would have them do to you" (Luke 6:31).

All Jesus' commands can be reduced to his one, new, commandment. In other words, what Moses was inspired to do in the old covenant, Jesus did in the new; he put morality *in the framework* of the new covenant between Father and Son. "As the Father loves me, so I have loved you. As I have loved you, so love one another". The new covenant is, "I will be your *Abba*, you will be my child". The human morality that flows from the covenant is always seen in terms of *"Thank you,* Father. How can I imitate

88

you, to please you in return?" Every moral command of Christ fits that picture.

As the new covenant fulfils and perfects the old, so the new morality fulfils and perfects the old. But neither Jesus nor Moses brought new instructions — only a new framework. Christians will, however, be more likely than most to have a consistent morality, since whatever they do will relate to the one God (Good) as *Abba*.

Hence Jesus leaves it to his followers, once they know God as Father, to decide for themselves what is right: "And why do you not judge for yourselves what is right?" (Luke 12:57).

•

Not just any kind of morality

Even though the teachings of Jesus and his church do not provide ready-made answers from God to human dilemmas and problems, christian moral teaching will not fit in with just any kind of well-meaning humanist morality. There are two levels to watch: one, the deepest idea of what we mean by goodness, or who we think God is; the other, how best to reflect that same goodness in our lives, in the choices directly in front of us. Christians can and will differ from many non-christian thinkers as regards what Good is, and will differ even among themselves as to the best way of expressing that goodness in our own human lives.

The God that Jesus revealed has a universal love, excluding no man, woman or child that ever lived or lives or will live. Those who knew God in the days of the Old Testament seem often to have thought of him as being exclusive and choosy: God is the father of Israel, so if you are a good Israelite then you are under the fatherhood of God. You have to be a good Israelite first, and there of course is the rub.

For Jesus, on the other hand, you do not have to be a good anything to come under the fatherhood of God; you just have to be, to exist, and God loves you as your personal *Abba*. So any system of morality which puts the good of the majority or the good of the state as the ultimate Good is inconsistent with Jesus' teaching. If the ship of state sails away and leaves even one behind, if the state decides that one must die for the good of the people, if the state or the church or any other organisation decides to settle for the ninety-nine sheep who conform and to leave even one behind, then the system is less than christian. Jesus makes quite clear that as long as we leave behind even the least of the undesirables, we leave Jesus behind (cf. Matthew 25:31-46).

●

"If you love me . . ."

Above all, morality is free. "*If* you love me, you will keep my commandments" (John 14:15). If, however, we do not love Jesus, it does not stop him from loving us. We do not earn his love by our good behaviour, but by being his Father's children, which depends not on our own efforts but on our Father's choice.

●

Where do laws come from?

Laws are formed by the pooling of a community's experience of following its conscience. Men and women in a community discover that certain forms of action lead to desirable results for the community, certain others lead to bad consequences; so they create laws to encourage the good and discourage the bad. There are laws at family, local, national and international level, depending on how wide the community in question happens to be. But the laws are the distillation of past experience. They can never be held more sacred than present experience, since the only authority (from God) for the laws comes precisely from experience.

Similarly with church laws. Their authority stems from the experience of previous generations of christians reflecting in the Spirit on what they judged to be right, for instance in the light of what the consequences turned out to be. Take the matter of attendance at the Sunday Eucharist. The foundation for the law now existing in the catholic church, that all members must attend, is based on the experience of past generations, that if one did not attend regularly, one lost touch with the community (and therefore with Christ) and began to lose hope in Christ's promises. So, to guide future generations away from the heartbreak of finding out the hard way by bitter experience, yesterday's experience is codified in a law demanding weekly attendance.

Any law is only as sound as the reasons for putting it on the statute book. The fact that a law has been there as long as anyone can remember does not lend it any authority once experience shows good reasons for now removing the law. "The sabbath was made for man, not man for the sabbath", said Jesus (Mark 2:27). Laws are for men, not men for laws. If the conscience of my forefathers says one thing (preserved in the law) and my conscience or our conscience today says another thing quite different, then I am bound to follow today's conscience rather than the law, since the only authority of the law is that it was once "today's conscience", that it was once "today's link with the Father's will".

●

Not "situation ethics"

"Situation ethics" would hold that if you see a certain line of action as right, and I see it as wrong, then we may both be correct. The catholic tradition of ethics would

91

hold, on the contrary, that we cannot both be right. One of us is bound to be mistaken — perhaps you, perhaps me — if we flatly contradict one another. There is only one God and Father. The way forward is through moral discussion and argument, but in the meantime you must do what you see to be right, whereas I must avoid doing it if I see it as wrong.

How can the one God lead you and me to his one truth along different paths? How can obedience to an erroneous conscience ever be the best way to the light? One scriptural example may be quoted, the case of Abraham, "our father in faith". Abraham is pictured as first of all thinking that God was asking him for the human sacrifice of his son Isaac. At the last minute it dawned upon Abraham that God wanted no such terrible tribute, and he substituted a ram instead (Genesis 22:1-14). The Book of Genesis describes the incident as a test, as if Abraham had to show his willingness to follow his conscience and do what he believed God to be asking (in accordance with local religious custom), before God could enlighten him that in fact he desired no such thing. The search for God which the children of Abraham pursued all through the Old Testament presents us with a long series of corrections and refinements of what had been sincerely held before. The debate of ethics takes place not only between two people, but also within individual persons (and communities) as they develop.

So how can obedience to an erroneous conscience ever be the best way to the light? The answer, however mysterious, is in the very bones of the Old Testament as it leads on to the New. The story of Abraham's race does not apologise for the false alleys the people explored in their search for the will of God. They even reckoned that God had called them up the blind alleys, before letting them see the true way. These, in fact, are among the "men of good will" who find God's "peace on earth". God can do what he wants with anyone whose heart is in the right place, and whose only desire is to please him.

THE CHURCH AND AUTHORITY

The Pope and morality

The First Vatican Council (1870) claimed that the Pope is infallible, i.e., cannot make a mistake, when as shepherd and teacher of all christians he defines a doctrine concerning faith or morals, to be held by the whole church. However, in practice the church has never claimed any ethical pronouncement of the Pope as being infallible. Possibly the reason is that the only ethical teachings which are infallibly right are so general as to be by now almost self-evident: like, "Do unto others as you would have them do to you".

The Pope's ethical teachings have, however, a special authority stemming from his position as the sign of unity in the church. He is in a unique position to say back to the church everywhere what he knows, from his contacts, the Spirit is saying in the consciences of its members. Similarly, in varying degrees, Bishops in Council with the Pope, Bishops in their own local groupings and their own dioceses, Bishops in Synod, priests in their parish or other work, priests in council, lay commissions and councils, parents, teachers, councils of religious . . . every grouping of christians has its own authority, wider or narrower depending on how attuned it is to hear what the Spirit is saying in the consciences of the members of the church today.

Even the Pope cannot tell me what I think I ought to do. Only God can tell me that.

●

The Pope and faith

In exact parallel, the Pope is in a unique position to say back to the church what the faith of the church already is. This power of infallibility, as defined and limited above, some recent Popes have explicitly claimed to apply to certain dogmas as defined by themselves. Even then, they were careful to make thorough enquiry first, as to how widespread the belief in question was (e.g., Pope Pius XII and the doctrine of the Assumption of Mary, 1950), and how ancient the belief was, before giving it back to the church as an integral part of what was already believed.

The Pope could not suddenly expect the church to believe in a Fourth Person on a par with Father, Son and Holy Spirit, because he can only define what the faith of the church already is.

Even the Pope cannot tell me what I believe, though by virtue of his position he can say what "we believe".

●

The Pope and unity

The role of the Pope, then, whom catholics see as the successor of St Peter, is by no means to *replace* my conscience or our conscience. Nor is it to *replace* my faith or our faith. Nonetheless, his role has to do with conscience and faith, because of his position as sign of unity.

There is only one God. The perfect sign or incarnation of God is one person: Jesus Christ. We are the church, not at the expense of the individual person, but only to cherish individual persons. God is shepherd, Christ is shepherd, Peter is shepherd, the Pope is shepherd, you and I are shepherd. God is light, Christ is light, Peter is light, the Pope is light, you and I are light. God is rock, Christ is rock, Peter is rock, the Pope is rock, you and I are rock. God never sacrifices one for the good of the ninety-nine. The world does that, but God does not do that.

A body has only one head. A tree has one main trunk. A building has one foundation stone. An arch has one cornerstone. A boat has only one helmsman. Once we all depended on Peter's faith, without which Jesus would have died in vain, unrecognised as the Christ, the Son of God. Now the world depends on one man, in that if we cannot all find common cause with one man, we can never make one world. The Pope stands as a living reminder to the world of the words of Christ, "As long as you did it to the least of my little ones, you did it to me" (Matthew 25:40). The Pope is "the least of the little ones", "the servant of the servants". If we all sail away together but leave the Pope behind, we have left Jesus behind . . . and the shepherd, and the light, and the rock.

The function of the Pope has to be something that does not depend on his human ability or powers. His office must be able to survive wicked Popes, unwise Popes, worldly Popes, senile Popes, as well as wise and holy Popes. The main thing he does (however humiliating the thought) is simply to be there, "the least of the brethren", with whom we all have to come to terms.

●

How could Jesus be so sure?

How could Jesus be so sure that his message would survive his death? Even allowing for the possibility that the gospel writers have read back into the words of Jesus of Nazareth many things that only became clear after the resurrection, there is still an unmistakable sureness in the sayings of Jesus. A parable like the one just quoted, about the king saying "As long as you did it to the least of my little ones, you did it to me" — Jesus identifying himself with the plight of every man born or to be born

97

— indicates either an almighty gamble or an inner knowledge. What was it Jesus knew, to make him so sure?

First and foremost, he knew his message was from God. He knew he was right to call God *"Abba!"* and to invite the rest of us. Prophets, and men and women who pray, have always been able to recognise the signature of God in certain truths that dawned upon them. Jesus was one of those prophets, but with a conviction about a truth uniquely his own, which had never dawned on any other prophet.

Secondly, we should remember Jesus' "seed" parables, against the background of this quotation from Isaiah, certainly well known to Jesus:

> For as the rain and the snow come down from heaven
> and return not thither but water the earth
> making it bring forth and sprout
> giving seed to the sower and bread to the eater,
> so shall my word be that goes forth from my mouth;
> it shall not return to me empty,
> but it shall accomplish that which I purpose
> and prosper in the thing for which I sent it.
>
> (Isaiah 55:10f.)

The first letter of St Peter is not going beyond the meaning of Jesus when it says the seed is the word of God by which we are born again (cf. 1 Peter 1:23ff.), the word by which God calls us his children and we call him *"Abba!"* Jesus knew that in him God had spoken a word, and that it would not return to God empty.

Thirdly, Jesus had witnessed at Caesarea Philippi God revealing to Peter that the hope of all the ages was contained in the person and message of himself, Jesus of Nazareth. When Peter said, "You are the Christ", Jesus was able to face Jerusalem and death with a certain serenity, because the seed had already taken root in someone other than himself (cf. Mark 8:27-31).

98

Fourthly, Jesus knew that his word was not even completely spoken yet. He had still to love his own to the bitter end, so that his disciples would see in him how God loves his own right to the bitter end. Then, in God's providence, Peter would believe the content of the message, the hidden mystery, as well as believing that Jesus was the Christ.

The sureness of the church about its message and mission has the same foundation as Jesus' sureness.

●

Anointing

Four of the seven sacraments of the church use the symbolism of anointing: baptism, confirmation, ordination and the anointing of the sick. The latter relies on the symbolism of oil or chrism as an ointment, as it is used by doctors on their patients or by athletes on themselves.

For the sacraments of baptism, confirmation and ordination, the main symbolism of chrism is "choice" and "royalty". In baptism we celebrate the fact that God chooses us as his royal children, and never, never goes back on his choice. In confirmation we celebrate the fact that God chooses to call us to be like him, and never ceases to call us no matter how many times we shut our ears. In ordination we celebrate the fact that the seed of God's word does not just blow at random round the world but is sent with chosen sowers, to the ends of the earth and until the end of time. The success of the seed depends not on human qualities, but on God's choice.

●

Character of three sacraments

These three sacraments, of baptism, confirmation and ordination, are by their very nature given only once. In picture-language, we could say that the baptised person has his or her own place at the Father's table, which can never be taken away. The person confirmed has his or her own chalice, his or her own cup of suffering and glory, presented to him daily. The person ordained has his (not her?) seed for the sowing, is chosen and sent out. God never needs to send out his word twice, because it is always effective the first time of sending.

(To speak in a parable of my own, if there were only one christian left on earth, that person would be the successor of St Peter, a rock, a lighthouse, the helmsman, the shepherd, the sower. For the word "Christ" means "anointed" just as the word "messiah" means "anointed", and every anointed christian is another Christ. Modern human biology gives added point to St Paul's saying that the church is the body of Christ. Every single cell in a human body has within it the whole range of that body's characteristics. Each cell is a microcosm of the whole body. My fingers know if my eyes are blue. Likewise each christian has the complete range of Christ's characteristics, each christian is another Christ.)

The character of baptism is, that it gives the candidate a permanent right to the bread of the children; the character of confirmation is, that it gives the candidate the right to the chalice. The character of ordination is, that it gives the candidate the right to preside at the Eucharist of bread and chalice, presenting to each generation, everywhere, the gift of God and the call of God.

●

Where is Jesus Christ?

Jesus Christ is Lord, at the right hand of God the Father. Wherever God may be found, there Jesus Christ may be found. Since God may be found wherever we are, so may Jesus Christ be found wherever we are. Since God

100

may be found wherever life exists, so Jesus Christ may be found wherever life exists. Moreover, since Jesus Christ is our mediator, our "Joseph" between us and God, whenever and wherever we find God we find him through Jesus.

Jesus tells us he may be found in the hungry, the thirsty, the stranger, the naked, the sick and the prisoner (cf. Matthew 25:31-46). Whatever we do to them, we do to him, he implies. Elsewhere, he adds little children to the list: "Whoever receives one such child in my name, receives me" (Mark 9:37). Every human being is created in the likeness of God, and is therefore a sign of Christ, who is the living image of his Father.

The Second Vatican Council tells us of four ways Jesus is present at the celebration of the Eucharist: in the person of the minister of the sacrament, in the "gathering of two or three" or more, in the word of God spoken in the scriptures, and in a unique way in the bread and wine of the sacrament.

The same or similar four ways of presence may well be sought and found in the other six of the church's sacraments. In each sacrament there is a minister, not always ordained, but Christ is present in the minister just the same. In marriage the ministers are the husband and wife, and they remain so until death parts them. In each sacrament there is a gathering of at least two or three in Christ's name, so Christ is there on that account. In each sacrament the scriptures are read, so Christ is there speaking. In each sacrament there is a particular presence of Christ which depends on the meaning of the signs — Christ adopting us in baptism, Christ calling us in confirmation, Christ feeding us and sealing our everlasting covenant in the Eucharist, Christ bringing us God's forgiveness in reconciliation, Christ caring for our sickness in the anointing of the sick, Christ loving us "unto death" in marriage, Christ "always and everywhere" in ordination.

101

When Christ is present, he is not "partly present", since he is one person and cannot be divided. The different signs are doorways to the one presence. Our eyes are clouded, veiled, but if and when the veil is lifted even slightly we become aware of the whole Christ along with, and through, the particular aspect we are approaching him from. Christ is one jewel of many facets.

Catholics have found particularly helpful the "living and abiding presence" of Christ in the eucharistic species of bread and wine, reserved originally for the communion of the sick, but for many centuries now reserved also for contemplation and worship.

Since every christian is anointed another Christ, Christ is present in each of us all the time. We pray to Christ such prayers and hymns as "Take my hands and make them as your own". When I respond to God's adoption and pray *"Abba!* Father!", the Spirit of Christ is answering in me. When I respond to God's call and imitate my Father's ways, I am another Christ doing his work with my hands. He uses my eyes to look, my ears to hear, my lips to speak and pray, my hands to heal and help, my feet to go looking for his lost sheep. He and I are one — one body, one shepherd, one rock, one light.

Whenever two or three are gathered in the name of Christ, he is there in the midst of them (cf. Matthew 18:20), not only when one of the seven sacraments of the church is being celebrated. Whenever the scriptures are read and pondered, Christ is speaking. The very presence of the book of the scriptures in writing deserves a reverence somehow akin to the reverence we give to the presence of Christ in the reserved Eucharist — the power is, so to speak, dormant even when the book is not being read. The words live too in our memory once we have heard them, and they slot into place over the years as our minds and hearts feed on them.

The presence of Christ in sacramental ministers and preachers also abides beyond the mere performance of rituals. There is an abiding presence of Christ with husband

and wife throughout marriage. There is an abiding presence of Christ in the hierarchical church structures linked to ordination. There is a special sign of Christ's presence in whoever succeeds to the role of Peter, in whoever succeeds to the role of the apostles (bishops, each a patriarch of one of the tribes of the new Israel), in whoever is ordained to minister to the local church, and in all their gatherings and communications.

Whenever we forgive one another's sins and faults — seven times in the day even a good man has sins to forgive — Christ is there, inside or outside the sacrament of reconciliation.

The church of Jesus' disciples, wherever and however it exists, is a living and effective sign of his presence. Whenever we gather in his name, he, the shepherd, is there gathering us.

●

"Better for you that I go away"

When we consider this quite wonderful closeness of Christ to each christian, we can understand the saying of Jesus in St John's gospel, that it was better for him to go away, so that the Counsellor would come to us (cf. John 16:7). As long as Jesus was with us in the flesh, then the answer to the question, "Where is Jesus?" was a simple statement of physical fact: "Jesus is in Bethany at the house of Martha and Mary", or "Jesus is in Jericho" or "Jesus is in Jerusalem, at the Beautiful Gate of the temple".

Only since the resurrection, and the coming of the Spirit to the church, has it been possible to give such enormously rich and varied answers to the same question.

●

Beloved disciple

The church, filled with the Spirit of Christ, thus becomes the sacrament or sign to the world which Jesus was in the days when he was with us "in the flesh". Jesus knew that every man alive should hear the message he brought us from God, every person alive both then and in the future, and indeed the men of the past. He was commissioned to send messengers out in his turn, because of the universal nature of the message and the fact that no one else was preaching it. He knew God as *"Abba!"*; no one else had ever preached this; so Jesus would have to send out disciples, in his time and after his time.

"I am the light of the world" becomes "You are the light of the world". "As the Father sent me, I send you". As the Son is in the bosom (John 1:18) of the Father, so the beloved disciple is in the bosom of Christ (John 13:23). The Son tells what he sees of God, and puts flesh on what he sees. Now the church (you and I) sees what the world does not see, namely the presence of God in Christ, and puts what it sees into flesh and blood, words and actions. Then "whoever receives you, receives me; whoever receives me, receives not me but him who sent me". "The Father chose me, to go out and bear fruit. I choose you, to go out and bear fruit" (cf. John 15:1-17).

The disciple must be loved first, and know that he is beloved. Then, and only then, can he mediate the same love to others. Jesus is baptised, before he is transfigured. The christian is baptised, before he is confirmed. The christian takes the bread of the children, before accepting the chalice. The gift of God comes first, before he calls us to take his likeness to others.

St Ignatius of Antioch, who was bishop there so shortly after St Peter the Apostle, says, "Take a fresh grip on your faith (the very flesh of the Lord) and your love (the life-blood of Jesus Christ)". Elsewhere he says, "I am fain for the bread of God, even the flesh of Jesus Christ, who is the seed of David, and for my drink I crave that blood of his which is love imperishable" (Ignatius *To the Trallians* 8; *To the Romans* 7).

MARY, MODEL OF THE CHURCH

"Behold your Mother"

The "beloved disciple", who usually stands for the reader
and not just for the source and writer of St John's gospel,
finds himself not only "in the bosom" of Christ, but
also at the foot of the cross. "When Jesus saw his mother
and the disciple whom he loved standing near, he said
to his mother, 'Woman, behold, your son!' Then he said
to the disciple, 'Behold, your mother!' And from that
hour the disciple took her to his own home" (John
19:26f.).

That passage is one of the foundations in scripture for the
church's devotion to Mary as Mother of each disciple of
her son.

●

"Abba" not exclusively male

Even though the word *Abba* is at the very heart of our
christian religion, we should remember that like every
other word we speak about God it is a metaphor. When
we say *"Abba!"* to God we are making a real call to a
personal God, but the image in which we clothe our call
is a metaphor. God is not a human father. In fact, it
is nearer the truth to say God is not like a human father
than it is to say he is like a human father. Nevertheless,
"Father", especially the intimate word *"Abba"* is the
nearest we can get to a true picture, according to our
teacher, the Christ (Matthew 23:8-10).

Every reality and every image finds its source in God,
as rays come from the sun. We could say with St Paul that

all human fatherhood is called after God's fatherhood. But God the Father is not a man, nor is he a male, and any male image is for that reason as well inadequate. "Mother" is another picture of God that the scriptures use, though nothing like as frequently as "Father". "Will a mother forget her child?" asks Isaiah. "Even if she did, I will never forget you" (cf. Isaiah 49:14ff.).

For all too many children suffering the separation of their parents, their mother has to become their whole security, and "Mum" means as much to them as "Mum and Dad", "Mummy and Daddy", "Mother and Father" means to children with united parents. Even in many marriages which survive, the children see chiefly in their mother the characteristics of unquestioning love and endless faithfulness which we ascribe to God.

Jesus compares himself to a mother hen: "O Jerusalem! How often would I have gathered your children together as a hen gathers her brood under her wings, and you would not" (Matthew 23:37).

What is more, the Church, upon which falls the vocation of showing God to the world today, is described in almost exclusively female images: mother, city, temple, boat, bride, building.

●

Male and female

"So God created man in his own image, in the image of God he created him; male and female he created them" (Genesis 1:27). As in the creation, so it goes in the re-creation of mankind through Christ. Christ does not reach to the ends of time and the ends of the earth except through his church. The likeness to God is not entirely contained in the male image of Christ, nor entirely in the female image of the church, but in the fusion of the

108

two. Christian marriage, according to St Paul, is a great mystery, "and I take it to mean Christ and the church" (Ephesians 5:32).

It stands to reason that any woman may hope to be better equipped than any man to demonstrate the "femaleness" of God, who is the origin of those qualities which complement and complete "maleness". Mary does not have to work very hard at looking more like a mother than her son ever could.

●

Mary, Model of the Church

Mary is often called "the model of the church". That is to say, we can look at Mary and see clearly in one person the characteristics that should be in the community of the church. Thus we, as a church, have a model to imitate and to turn to for inspiration.

Of necessity, there is no limit to the thoughts and inspirations mankind may have in looking at Mary in the light of the scriptures and of tradition, but the thoughts usually centre round a few key moments in her life-story.

"Hail, full of grace" is the greeting of the angel Gabriel (Luke 1:28): "Greetings, you who are all gift". Nothing in Mary is of her own. Everything she has is given to her, and she knows it. She is a "serving-girl", "of low degree", "hungry" and "poor", and she only deserves to be called blessed because of the great things God has done for her (Luke 1:46-55). In this she is the model of the church, which is the community of those who accept the gift of being God's children. Then, too, she is like that other image of the church, "the holy city, the new Jerusalem, coming down out of heaven from God", which is another way of saying the same thing, "full of grace".

Mary gave Christ to the world. The church gives Christ to the world today. Physical motherhood was not thought of by Jesus as being any great thing of itself to boast of. When a woman in the crowd around him called blessings on the womb that bore him and the breasts he had sucked, Jesus replied, "Blessed rather are those who hear the word of God and keep it!" (Luke 11:28). Physical nearness of itself does not always lead to conversion: we have only to think of the many people who daily met Jesus in the temple and yet were willing to see him crucified. At the same time, Jesus is in fact praising his mother, since she of all people did hear the word of God and keep it. This too is what the church should be doing: hearing the word of God ("You are my beloved child . . ."); and keeping it: giving the world God's word made flesh, giving the world love in action to look at and be hopeful, in the midst of sorrow.

Tradition has seen another role shared by Mary and the church in the story of the marriage feast at Cana. Jesus is there alerted to the needs of the wedding guests by his mother: "They have no wine" (John 2:3). Many times Jesus said to his disciples that they could ask, together, for anything at all in his name and his Father would give it to them. Mary is our model as regards asking.

Mary presenting Jesus to God in the temple, Mary treasuring what she sees and hears in her heart, Mary hurrying to help Elizabeth in her need, Mary standing to watch God's love shown in Jesus on the cross, Mary waiting with the apostles and disciples for the Spirit . . . in these and other scenes Mary on her own shows what we together should be doing.

●

Pruning

Jesus often compares human life and growth to the growth of plants and trees. Taking a few of these comparisons together, we can say that you and I, singly or with one another, are like a tree, like a vine, say. Left to ourselves, we grow wild, and produce sour grapes, useful to nobody. The Father of Jesus is the vinedresser, the one who loves and prunes and tends the vine. Once a tree is adopted by God, he prunes it and cares for it, and it produces plentiful grapes for wine-making.

●

Nature and grace

The word "natural" is ambiguous in christian tradition. A tree left to itself naturally produces sour grapes — so nature is bad; but a tree pruned by the Father naturally produces wine in plenty — so nature is good. Often we contrast "nature" and "grace" as though they were something completely at odds, but we should remember that God calls forth *the good that is in us*. The "gift" or "grace" is like the pruning or loving care given by a gardener, to bring out the good that is naturally in us.

Even the goodness in our nature is a gift of God, so we do not have anything here to boast of. However, the importance of clinging to the belief that nature can be good (if pruned by the Father) is that the best traditions of christianity have insisted that the human heart is to be trusted. Once assured that God is my Father and has his pruning-knife at the ready, I may follow my heart, search after my deepest desires, and do what I will. "Love God, and do what you will".

When we think of human nature in the light of this image of the vine, we can see that God is not to blame for any "original sin" or "warped nature" in man. There is nothing wrong with the tree. But the tree is free to give itself to the vinedresser or not, free to let itself be pruned and be fruitful, or else to be untended and to yield sour grapes. Another way the parables sometimes express the

111

same truth is that the stewards of the vineyard refuse to give the produce to the owner. Again, there is nothing wrong with the vineyard.

●

Conceived without sin

One of the traditions about Mary holds that she was conceived without original sin. This search into christian doctrine has now provided a framework against which to understand a little that doctrine, so strange at first sight. Obviously, original sin is not detectable by science at the moment of conception, so what does the doctrine of "immaculate conception" mean?

I said earlier on that "original sin" is the name we give to the state of those who do not dare to call God "*Abba!* Father!" People in the state of original sin do not dare to believe that the gates of heaven are as wide open as a father's arms are open to welcome his child. Very well, then: in saying Mary was conceived without original sin we are saying that Mary was always prepared to trust God as her Father, even though she only explicitly began to do so once Jesus had explicitly taught her. St Luke's gospel shows her puzzlement when she complains to Jesus, "Your father and I have been looking for you anxiously", and he replies that he had to be about his Father's business (Luke 2:41-50). Mary and Joseph "did not understand the saying", but she "kept all these things in her heart".

Mary was always prepared to trust God as her Father. We have the evidence of scripture to make this seem a reasonable statement. The greeting of the angel calls her "graced", "all-given-to", and the prayer put on her lips by St Luke is completely devoid of self-centredness. She did not know the secret of the Good News, but she was completely prepared for it.

If we express the Good News in secular language, we would say that "Reality is friendly", or "Life at the deepest level can be trusted", or "The truth can be trusted as a friend". Anyone "without original sin" just has to be a very trusting person. And child-care experts stress the vital importance of the first two years of life, the moment of birth, the time of the mother's pregnancy, and even the circumstances under which a child is conceived: everything has to be right, the child has to be wanted, secure, treasured, the first sight of it awaited, the new baby bonded to its mother, and loved and cuddled and cherished by both parents, before we have a completely trusting child. Naturally speaking, Mary could not have grown up sinless, completely trusting, not having the root of sin (which is fear of God as a taskmaster) in her, unless her beginnings were surrounded by quite outstanding parental love. Traditionally, then, we honour Joachim and Anne as her parents.

Taking the other image of nature and grace, the vine untended producing sour grapes and the vine tended by the Father producing grapes for wine, what does the Immaculate Conception of Mary mean in those terms? Mary was a vine never untended, but always under the watchful care of the Father. Since God's care is shown to us through other people, again we come back to the love her parents must have given her from the first moment of her existence. A tree only grows so noble and fruitful when it has received a proper start in life.

Another major witness to the specialness of Mary is the unspoken evidence of the kind of person Jesus is seen to be in the gospels. Such a son must have had a very special mother, as the nameless woman in the crowd so truly commented (Luke 11:28). We have every reason to believe that Mary was far more than a physical presence to Jesus, and was his mother in things of the spirit as well as in things of the body.

●

The sinlessness of Jesus and Mary

Jesus who frees us from sin was himself sinless (e.g., Hebrews 4:15). His consciousness of God his Father's love for him must have been total. He was completely "beloved", and knew it, and so could love completely. Since his knowledge of God as *"Abba!"* was something entirely special to himself in the history of the human race (we only share it by courtesy of Jesus, not *vice versa*), we are within our rights to guess that his consciousness of God's love for him was unique. The one whose faith is so complete that he "sees" is every bit as free as the one who acts on a more obscure faith, so Jesus was still free and could be tempted.

Jesus' consciousness of being loved must have come to him initially through Mary and Joseph, and especially through Mary in the very early stages of his human life. For any baby the mother's love is the first and most crucial factor in development. Catholics argue back from Jesus' sinlessness, to his consciousness of being loved by God first, to the perfect love his parents (and especially Mary) always gave him from the first moment of his conception, to Mary's own sinlessness, to *her* being so loved and tended that she never used her freedom to sin.

Why stop at Mary? How did Mary turn out to be so completely loving, unless her parents were so in their turn? And if that was the case, were Joachim and Anne not "conceived without sin" as well? The teaching of the church takes the sequence no further back than Mary, and calls this a unique or "singular" privilege given to her. Anyone can agree that Jesus was totally beloved by Mary. Anyone can agree that the history of the human race in the era before Christ shows human kind as very much a mixture of good and bad, corn and weeds, sheep and goat, in fact the same sort of mixture we are today. How did the parent stock of Jesus come to be so perfect that no flaw appears in him? To protect our conviction that Jesus is flawless, we insist that Mary too was totally loved, totally trusting, and hence totally loving.

The Virgin Mary

Christian tradition holds that Mary was a virgin all her days, and that Joseph her husband had no part in the conception of her son Jesus.

Even here, there is something for our imitation and reflection: the doctrine is not just a useless piece of mental furniture. The main effect and perhaps the main purpose of the tradition is to preserve the unique relationship between Jesus and his Father in heaven. Where we can imitate is by each of us learning to appreciate our own unique relationship with our adoptive *Abba,* which is as special to you and me as our own thumbprint is special to us, our own name is special to us (Revelation 2:17), our own glory is special to us (1 Corinthians 15:41), our own baptism is special to us, our own conscience is special to us.

Jesus is not the only one, now, who can say to an earthly father: "Did you not know I must be about my Father's business?", since Jesus tells us to call no man on earth father, as we have one Father, who is in heaven (Matthew 23:9).

●

The Assumption

Catholic tradition also holds that what God did for Jesus in the resurrection, he has done for Mary as well, whether or not there were any witnesses. In this tradition Mary is once again the model of the church, since all of us are called to share the risen glory of Jesus Christ, the Son of God.

Jesus' glory is his own, as the one and only Son. Mary's glory, like ours, is always reflected glory. If he is like the sun, she is like the moon.

THE SPIRIT AT WORK

Fruit of the Spirit

St Paul tells us, "The fruit of the Spirit is love, joy, peace, patience, kindness, goodness, faithfulness, gentleness, self-control" (Galatians 5:22ff.). The Spirit is still the same Spirit by which we cry out *"Abba! Father!"*

Once we know that God is our loving and personal Father, we live in love and try to pass that love on to others, loving him in them in return for his great love for us. Once we are securely built on the rock of his love, we can afford to be joyful, because nothing can take away our treasure. Once the central anxiety of our human lives is allayed by the knowledge that the ever-living God has forgiven us, then we can live in peace and show by our forgiveness of others the kind of God we believe in. And so on. Each "fruit" is directly related to the Spirit of our Father's love for us and Christ's love in return.

●

Peace, or division?

According to John's gospel, Jesus left his peace to his disciples as a bequest in his last will and testament (cf. John 14:27). According to Luke's gospel, Jesus says "Do you think that I have come to give peace on earth? No, I tell you, but rather division", especially division within families (cf. Luke 12:49-53). How are we to reconcile these sayings which seem to contradict one another?

119

The truth brought by Jesus means that human clannish-
ness is not enough. Families cling together; "birds of a
feather flock together"; we love people of our own kind,
our own colour, our own country, our own background.
We form cliques and clubs, and put up "Members only"
notices. "Not good enough", says Jesus. "You are all
members of the one family, and therefore no one is to
be excluded". Once a disciple has been inspired by Jesus,
he will cause division in the family or the cliques he
used to belong to. His new, wider, vision will be seen by
some of his former relations or friends as a betrayal. "What
do you mean by supporting a foreigner, a stranger, all
those sick and undesirable people? Stay with us, support
your own kind, and we will support you". Hence comes
division, and not the peace which formerly existed inside
the security of the "Members only" enclosure.

The peace that Jesus gives is quite different. It is the
peace that comes of knowing God as my *Abba*.

●

Living water

"Whoever drinks of the water that I shall give him will
never thirst; the water that I shall give him will become
in him a spring of water welling up to eternal life" (John
4:14). What did Jesus mean by this "water" he would give?
Is it exactly the same as is meant by the waters of baptism,
which we do not drink?

The living water given by Jesus is the truth, which we
"drink in" as dry ground drinks in the rain, that God is
our Father and loves us with an everlasting love. With this
knowledge, and our acceptance of it, which is faith, we
become like a city with its own water supply within the
city walls. No matter what enemies lay siege to us, we
can withstand their assaults year after year, because we

have our own living water, our own spring or well of fresh water to keep us alive and hopeful.

In terms of the "seed" and "plant" and "tree" parables used by Jesus, the seed is the faith of a disciple, faith which grows into fruitful love; and what waters the plant is, again, the truth that God is my *"Abba!"*

●

Baptism of desire

Not only christians have the Spirit of God; not only christians can be freed from original sin and become fruitful. Wherever the fruit of the Spirit is found, there we can be sure that the Father is at work pruning and dressing the vine. Not only christians can believe that God is incurably friendly, that reality is hopeful and that the truth is on the side of us sinners. God is not limited to working through his own church.

Those whom the Spirit enlightens without bringing them to christian baptism find themselves in a position similar to that of Mary the mother of Jesus, John the Baptist and countless others before Jesus began to teach: ready (each in their own degree) for the Good News, but most of them never living to hear it spelled out as Jesus spelled it out.

Christians find all other religious systems inadequate, because other religions stand for a different relationship with God from that which christians enjoy. If, however, others following what they see to be right in the framework of their own beliefs come to an understanding of reality scarcely distinguishable from our own, then christians may perhaps be forgiven for mentally "baptising" those others as virtual christians. "Your attitudes towards the deepest things in life are right" is what we are trying to say to them, wishing that their witness to the truth could be more closely and visibly linked to our own.

121

All men are saved by faith, faith in the love that others have shown them. All truly good works in this world are a response, a *Thank you*, for love that has been received. So all truly loving acts are built on grace, built on gift. "My parents loved me. Now they are gone, but I in my turn care for my children, not expecting any return". This is the normal pattern of salvation.

Faith and love are therefore basically the same for christians and for all others. Christian hope, however, is more special to christians. Our hope is in the resurrection of Jesus. Because of it we dare to believe in God's love for us and we dare to love others without expecting a return. No doubt God has his own ways of reassuring non-christians that love and goodwill are the only things that matter in the long run, for so many of them put us christians to shame by their unselfish love.

●

Faith and seeing

Faith in its full maturity can be almost the same as seeing. "You believe because you have seen me", says Jesus to Thomas (John 20:29a). No one could ever persuade the likes of St Teresa of Avila that Jesus is not alive and risen: she has seen him risen, and that is that. Her faith is like a rock, quite immovable. When faith reaches a stage of "seeing", it does not cease to be free. Jesus was free, and was truly tempted. A lover is more, not less, free to love his lass when he sees her.

What about Jesus' next saying to Thomas which follows in the same verse of John's gospel? "Blessed are those who have not seen and yet believe" (John 20:29b). The early steps of faith are nearly always steps in the dark. As children or as adults we see and experience the love and care of some at least of those who surround us. Part of what they say, in trying to explain to us the secret of their love, we can understand; part of it is beyond us. Blessed are those who take the hint, who follow the clues. We tend to believe what those who love us say, because we believe in, and trust, them. Only gradually do we come to understand more of the "secret" of their attraction for us, and begin to be able to reproduce it in our own lives. This is the way faith is sown, faith grows, and faith turns into love. Oddly enough, we come to realise that in trusting, we were trusting something or Someone we already knew, something or Someone we *recognised* in those we found attractive. "That way of life is true; it must be right; it chimes in with my very deepest instincts".

One definition of faith says that by it we "believe without doubting whatever God has revealed". This is not first and foremost a question of believing the articles of the Apostles' Creed, as the *Catechism of Christian Doctrine* led me to understand as a child, nor is it first and foremost a question of agreeing with official church documents. The basic place where God reveals to me, even as a child, is in my own heart, which tells me whom I can trust.

For this reason, the mentally handicapped usually find faith as readily as those who can reason better. One thing they nearly all know, and indeed they are experts at it, is whom to trust.

•

Faith moves mountains

"If you have faith as a grain of mustard seed, you will say to this mountain 'Move hence to yonder place', and it will move; and nothing will be impossible to you" (Matthew 17:20). How does faith move mountains, and what does Jesus mean?

Anxiety makes mountains out of mole-hills; faith makes mole-hills out of mountains. Anxiety magnifies small problems, and paralyses the fearful; faith in God's fatherly love makes large and very real problems seem insignificant. "God, who is the truth, thinks I am wonderful. So why should I break my heart over ill-health, bad luck, failure and disappointment? Only one thing matters, and I have it safe for ever: I can call God *'Abba!'* "

•

Mystery

A mystery is a truth about God which is so rich in meaning that we will never completely fathom it. The attempt to understand mysteries is very valuable. Indeed this little book is nothing else but an attempt to understand the christian mysteries.

•

The value of religion

The value of religion is that it gives meaning to life. In probing the mysteries of our religion we are constantly discovering *and recognising* the meaning of the lives we lead.

•

The narrow gate

There is a difficult saying of Jesus, "Enter by the narrow gate; for the gate is wide and the way is easy, that leads to destruction, and those who enter by it are many. For the gate is narrow and the way is hard, that leads to life, and those who find it are few" (Matthew 7:13f.).

Jesus lived and died to bring mankind the Good News about God. All the images he gives for his work involve "one" working for "the many". He on his own taught all men (before him, with him, after him) to call God *"Abba!"* and trust in his love. He is one seed dying to produce a hundredfold; he is one cornerstone for many living stones, for a whole temple; he is one light for all men; he is one shepherd for a hundred sheep; he is one boat for many passengers (and other boats besides are with him); he is one sower, sowing a field of grain; he is one loaf, feeding thousands; he is one chalice of the fruit of the vine, a precious ransom for many; he is one spring of living water, from which all who are thirsty can drink; he offers one sweet yoke to all who are burdened.

Could it not be that the one who enters by the narrow door saves those many who are taking the easy way out? Could it not be that Christ on the cross saves those many who are crucifying him? Could it not be that the right hand forgives the left hand for being so clumsy, and together they learn to live in God's peace? There seems to be a possibility that many people invest most of their heart and resources in things that perish, but do they invest their whole lives, their entire being? Could they not be like people who lose their whole house and its belongings in a fire, but themselves manage to escape in nothing more than what they stand up in? (cf. 1 Corinthians 3:15).

If they do, it will be because of the living example of Christ and "other Christs" who have voluntarily chosen to bear the burden of other people's indifference, who have chosen to be shepherds, lighthouses, lifeboats, fishers of men, foundation stones, servants, the grain that dies, the ransom. All these images belong first and properly to Christ, but also, with him and in him, to his disciples in his church, and to others who are "not far from the kingdom of God". We are called to enter the narrow door, in order to help save, in Christ, the rest of mankind. Christ, incarnate now in his disciples, is still the one who redeems.

●

Priesthood of the faithful; Priesthood of the ordained

All baptised christians are baptised as sheep of God's flock, but are called to be shepherds and to be "other Christs" for the rest of the world. This is the call we celebrate in the church's sacrament of confirmation. Christ becomes incarnate and active in every christian who responds to that call. Jesus as mediator between God and mankind becomes operative in all the active members of his church. In that sense, every baptised christian is called to share in the royal priesthood of Christ.

What is reserved to the ordained priesthood is best illustrated by what has been said above about the "character" of the sacrament of ordination, and also by what that sacrament celebrates.

In baptism christians are given each their own place at their Father's table. In confirmation each receives his or her own call to his or her own chalice. In the sacrament of ordination the candidate receives the right to preside at that same table: to say over the bread "This is my body" and present it to the children, to say over the chalice "This is my blood" and call the children each to their own share in the chalice. The guarantee is from God, not from the ordained ministers, that the bread and the wine will always be available. The seed or word of God once in the world will never die out, so in the ones who preside at the table rests the guarantee that the bread and wine, the faith and the love, the words and actions, the body and blood of Christ will remain available always and everywhere in the world.

If this word is to be *everywhere the same*, there must be one who presides above all at the table at any given time when the whole church assembles: this one we Catholics call the Pope. There is only one body, one spirit. If the word is to be the same *always*, there must be succession and ordination and commissioning, which makes the office of bishop necessary. The bishop will naturally be the one to preside if there is a local meeting of ordained ministers, and the one to make the main links between district and district, between his district and the Pope.

The eternal sacrifice of Christ is made sacramentally present especially through the words which only the priests say: "This is my body . . . "; "this is my blood". As if to say, "My body here, my blood there, the way it was when I showed you once for all how God loves you". The speaker is really Christ the high priest.

●

The problem of pain

The way of the cross, the way through the narrow door, the way of voluntarily doing without anything but God's fatherly love for me, is a painful way. Being a fully voluntary christian does not, however, mean volunteering for extra troubles from God. A man's riches perish with his bodily life, and a practising christian merely detaches himself from what he will have to lose anyway in the long run.

A christian does not expect more or less illness or misfortune because of being a christian. God does not distribute good health and good fortune as rewards for good behaviour, nor does he give out sickness and failure as punishments. That is the first thing to remember when we are afflicted with pain and distress. We are not being punished (cf. John 9:1-3).

Secondly, when we are in pain and distress we are taught by Jesus to pray exactly as he did: "My Father, if it be possible, let this cup pass from me; nevertheless, not as I will, but as thou wilt" (Matthew 26:39). Surely, if human parents can remove pain and sorrow from their child, they do. All the more surely, then, our heavenly Father would remove pain and sorrow from us his children if he could. I find it impossible to believe that my loving Father would let any of his children suffer needless pain. The only conclusion I can reach, when a child of God in pain has asked for the removal of pain "if it be possible" and the pain stays on, is that the removal was not possible. The Father could not have removed the cup of suffering from Jesus without acquiescing in a lie about himself and the truth. God cannot remove reality, he is the truth.

God cannot help it, if perishable things perish. But he does offer this naturally perishable creature his eternal friendship. The way in which the Father is all-powerful is the way in which love is all-powerful — to take us through all "the slings and arrows of outrageous fortune" still trusting that "all will be well" in his love, even though we die without any apparent relief. Jesus died so, and the resurrection was God's vindication of his trust.

Jesus tells us, moreover, to believe like sons and daughters, but to treat ourselves as servants and slaves of God, since God himself is like a servant. Thus it comes about that we thank God for the good things that come our way, but do not blame him for the evil that comes our way. A slave has no rights, so must be grateful for crumbs without demanding a loaf. Those who have the senses of hearing, speech, smell, taste and touch would not complain at not having sight, since they (and we who can see) have no right to be able to see. We can ask for it, but never demand it. "When you have done all you should do, say 'We are unprofitable servants' " (cf. Luke 17:10).

As old age or sickness come upon us, we can only say with Job, "The Lord has given, the Lord has taken away. Blessed be the name of the Lord" (Job 1:21). Only when we have lost everything will we be completely like God. "Father, into your hands I give my life" (cf. Mark 8:35; Luke 23:46).

●

Penance

St Ignatius of Loyola has a chilly description of penance. Taking no more than we strictly need, he says, of sleep, comfort, food and clothing is not penance but temperance. Penance means voluntarily having less than we need for good health of those and similar commodities.

The Sermon on the Mount advises us that prayer, fasting and almsgiving should all be done secretly (cf. Matthew 6:1-18). They should also be purely voluntary. God in no way demands penance from us his children. Repentance, yes, in the sense in which I have described repentance, as a turning of the heart to accept God as *Abba*. Penance, in the sense described above, never. That must be voluntary if undertaken at all.

How does penance fit in with the essential attitude to God as Father? It must never be allowed to threaten us, as if God were demanding a tribute of pain from his own children. So how does it belong in the christian life?

For a christian, for a child of God, morality is a *Thank you* to an over-generous Father. We believe we are his sons and daughters, but we treat ourselves as his servants, as Jesus taught us and showed us. The purpose of penance is to remind ourselves, because we want to remind ourselves, that we should not expect to be treated as princes and princesses yet. We want our *Thank you* to God to be generous, so we occasionally goad ourselves as if to say, "Fine servant you are! Swanning around expecting to be waited on, and fed, and kept in comfort while your betters need your services. For that, you can do without for a while!" Penance undertaken in that spirit can be a spur to doing greater things for God.

To make penance an end in itself would be crazy, and any form of competitiveness in works of penance is nonsense. All that the winner in such a competition could prove is "I am better at reproaching myself for being lazy than you are". Nor is penance to be lightly recommended to children or to beginners in the christian way of life, since the risk is too great that the beginner will think God is insisting on penance, and will begin to be scared of God. Jesus himself evidently gave his own disciples a holiday from fasting until such time as they might understand what the real purpose of penance is (cf. Mark 2:18-20).

A valuable form of penance quite frequently used in this country at the present time is to do without a meal and send the money to assist the hungry. This has the double effect of penance and almsgiving. To himself the one fasting says, "Fine brother you are, eating well every day while your brothers and sisters under the same sky are starving!"; and the money saved actually goes towards helping to feed them.

●

Rewards and punishments

God's love for us is undoubtedly free. Heaven is free, and not to be earned by good deeds. There are no rewards, exactly, for trusting that our benefactor really loves us.

Likewise there are no punishments, only consequences, as far as God is concerned. Reality is what it is, and we flaunt it at our peril.

Jesus advises us to be good and faithful servants. When the master returns and finds his servants doing as they should, they will be rewarded; when he finds them being irresponsible, they will be punished. These parables, however, must be taken in company with everything else Jesus teaches. We are not servants, we are children of God. Our service is voluntary, undertaken as a free *Thank you* to God who has loved us so much. Against that background, we goad ourselves to be good and faithful servants, we work *as if* for rewards and *as if* afraid of punishment for slacking, but believing all the time in our Father's love. Although living in the kingdom, we try not to be outdone by the children of "this generation" who slave away for money and for rewards. "Father, I am not worthy to be called your child. Let me be as one of your hired servants".

The give away line from Jesus on this matter of rewards and punishments is: "When you have done all that is commanded you, say, 'We are unworthy servants; we have only done what was our duty'". There can be no thanks from God, when the debt is still entirely on our side. All we have done by doing God's will is to express our thanks to him. He is not then obliged to thank us for saying *Thank you* to him.

Rewards are earned. We cannot earn God's fatherly love. So we cannot think of God's love as a reward. God loves us, and calls us to imitate him as our way of saying *Thank you*. Those who imitate him most closely learn to love without expecting thanks, since that is precisely the kind of love our God has.

Those who adore and imitate other gods reap the consequences, but are not being punished by the Father of Jesus. If any man or woman refuses to believe that reality is friendly, and either runs away or tries to compete and conquer, then that man or woman will find his own false version of reality crushing, and will be crushed by it unless he or she can learn to trust.

Just as there is no sense in competing with one another to see who can do the severest works of penance, so there is no sense in competing with one another in any other good works. At the end of the day all the winner of the competition can say is, "My *Thank you* card to our Father is more handsome than yours — bought with his money, of course".

To say all this is not to deny that we human beings have free will. God loves us, and we freely accept his love in faith. God calls us, and we freely try to please him by following our conscience in imitation of Jesus. God's love, our faith, God's call, and our good will are all of them gifts of God which leave us free. The saints of the Catholic church set great store by desires: "Have a great desire to serve God! Long to do great things for his kingdom!" In the end God does not so much reward our achievements as fulfil our desires.

●

Moral education

Does this mean that fear of punishment and hope of reward have no place in the moral education of christians?

A contemporary moral philosopher, Lawrence Kohlberg, suggests there are six stages in moral education: fear of punishment, hope of reward; loyalty to clique or family, loyalty to law; the ability to see exceptions to law, and lastly the seeing of morality as a unity beyond law. All human beings naturally start with fear: fear of being born, fear of the unknown, fear that the next meal may not arrive. They progress by stages towards a unified attitude to life which is no longer dependent on law.

An interesting facet of Kohlberg's findings is that people can only respond to appeals at their own level of morality or one stage ahead. Thus someone who is only behaving himself from fear of punishment will be able to respond to enticements of reward, but appeals to his sense of law and order will be useless.

Transferring such a theory of moral education and development into religious terms, we may see moral

132

development as the growth from fear to faith. The main point we should take is that there is absolutely no need to reinforce fear. Mankind starts with fear (which is, as I have suggested, the "original sin") and must be weaned away from it. Following Kohlberg's steps of progress, we could say that the learner is weaned away from fear first by hope of rewards, then weaned from hope of rewards by seeing the attractiveness of loyalty to the family and local groups, including the local religious group; then he progresses to loyalty to an international code of law and order including church laws, then to a stage where he can see exceptions to law and thus become part of the law-making process. Finally he reaches a stage where all life is integrated and law becomes like a pair of crutches that can be left aside. Kohlberg would say that very few people reach the final stage.

Jesus of Nazareth would be an obvious example of one who did reach the final stage. We see it at work in his way of relating all faith and all action to the one *Abba*. He is beyond the law (e.g., Mark 2:28), and yet is the fulfilment of the law (e.g., Matthew 5:17). He is the embodiment of what Jeremiah foretells when he says in the name of God: "I will put my law deep within them, and I will write it upon their hearts . . . There will be no further need for neighbour to teach neighbour, or brother to say to brother, 'Learn to know Yahweh!' No, they will all know me, the least no less than the greatest — it is Yahweh who speaks — since I will forgive their iniquity and never call their sin to mind" (Jeremiah 31:33f.).

This new covenant (cf. Jeremiah 31:31) is not confined to Jesus. Through him, with him and in him even the least of his brothers and sisters can reach the fullness of human moral development. The same Spirit is given to all.

●

133

Stewards of creation

The thought that mankind is the steward of all creation is not a new one, but is a thought which is both popular and necessary today. "Father, . . . you formed man in your own likeness and set him over the whole world, to serve you, his creator, and to rule over all creatures". This "stewardship" idea must never be allowed to obliterate the Good News. The heart of the matter is still that God is our *Abba*, saying to each one, "Reach for the stars, you who are my child; I will catch you if you fall". The owner is our Father; we try to behave like good stewards, but we must believe like children, both when we succeed in our stewardship and when we fail.

●

Poverty, chastity, obedience

Many religious orders and congregations exist whose members bind themselves by vows or solemn promises. Usually these vows are promises to observe poverty, chastity and obedience in accordance with the particular vision of christian service which was given to the founder or foundress. How do these three vows relate to the fatherhood of God?

The basis of all vows of poverty is something that every christian is called to: to have no other security but *Abba*, my Father in heaven.

Chastity as a religious vow is almost a sub-section of poverty. Non-possessive love and non-exclusive love becomes the mainspring of the one who vows chastity; he or she desires like Jesus to love everyone and possess no one. Marriage is a sign of the everlasting covenant, but it is not itself the everlasting covenant — only a sign. A person can find the reality, bypassing that sign.

Promises of poverty and chastity together make war on human ambition and the tendency to live for tomorrow. They leave, so to speak, nothing in a person's future for the flesh to look forward to. The result is, when all goes well and the promises were truly voluntary, that the person bound by vows of poverty and chastity has no worry about the past, since all is forgiven by our Father, and no plans for the future in which the heart is implicated, so the present moment, where God is, completely absorbs the heart and mind.

Vows of obedience differ from one religious order or congregation to the next. In general, a person entering religious life agrees to seek for the Father's will in the company of the others who live the same life, and in union with the church. It does not mean promising to go against my own conscience if the superior or community should require me to do something I see to be wrong. It may involve doing something I personally consider to be less wise. A religious brotherhood or sisterhood, like the church itself, has sometimes to take its time by the slowest, as a sign of unity. Progress which saves ninety-nine sheep and leaves one behind is no christian progress at all.

Deep down, therefore, the practice of poverty, chastity and obedience is no more than every christian is called to: reliance on God's love alone, non-possessive love for everyone in the world, the determination to leave no one behind.

There are no special rewards for those who take up and follow the religious life. Competition between those who follow different forms of religious life is nonsense.

GOD THE SON

God the Son

Eternity is not a long stretch of time. We tend to think of God enthroned before time and about to carry on being after time, whereas there is strictly speaking no such reality as "before time" and no such reality as "after time". Timelessness cannot be before or after anything. It simply is. The present moment we enjoy is a better picture of eternal life than any imagining of endless past or endless future. All times are present to God. When yesterday was Now, God was there. When tomorrow is Now, God will be there, ever the same. At the moment, God is here.

I suggested at the beginning of this book that the best way in to the mystery of Jesus as God the Son was to start with Jesus truly man reading off from his own heart what it means to be God's child. I too know now what it means to be God's child, but only by courtesy of Jesus. He seems to have known without any teacher.

We are not expected to believe that Jesus of Nazareth was sitting up there with the Father and the Spirit before time (there is no such reality as "before time") and that Jesus of Nazareth was consulted when the world was being created, and that one day the Father sent Jesus of Nazareth down to be born and to save mankind. Yet we are expected to believe that Jesus Christ is God the Son made man for us, that he is the Word of God incarnate, that he is the Second Person of the Blessed Trinity, that he is divine, that in a true sense we can say to him "My Lord and my God".

Apart from anything already contained in these pages, about Jesus as the mediator between God and man, the light from light, the way, and so on, is there anything else readily understandable that can be suggested now as a way in to the mystery of the divinity of Christ?

●

Pre-existence of Christ

The church teaching and the Fathers speak of the pre-existence of Christ, not the pre-existence of Jesus of Nazareth. That is the first thing to note and ponder. The Christ existed in God, the Word of God existed in God, the Son existed in God before Jesus of Nazareth was born.

The next thing to ponder is that you and I also existed in Christ before we were born. "Blessed be the God and Father of our Lord Jesus Christ, who has blessed us in Christ with every spiritual blessing in the heavenly places, even as he chose us in him before the foundation of the world, that we should be holy and blameless before him" (Ephesians 1:3f.). God chose us, you and me, in Christ before the foundation of the world. I can hear that and be deeply reassured, that God had me in mind from the beginning. If God had me in mind from the beginning of creation, then of course he had Jesus in mind, as the Christ, as the one in whom you and I would be saved. He had you and me in mind because of Jesus Christ the Lord.

●

The Wisdom of God

When the early Fathers of the church were living through the afterglow of the gospels, and coming to the formulation of the doctrine of the Trinity, they asked themselves, how could such a wonderful truth be hidden for so many centuries. We know from the writings of St Paul, and later St Irenaeus, that early christians searched the Old Testament for hidden references to the Son and the Spirit.

The Spirit was fairly easy to find, it was reckoned, since from the very first page "The Spirit breathed over the waters" in creation. The Son, it was thought, was to be found in the Old Testament chiefly in the references to the Wisdom of God, even though Wisdom in the Old Testament is usually spoken of in feminine images:

"For she is a breath of the power of God,
and a pure emanation of the glory of the Almighty;
therefore nothing defiled gains entrance into her.

For she is a reflection of eternal light,
a spotless mirror of the working of God,
and an image of his goodness".

(Wisdom of Solomon 7:25f.).

The Wisdom of God is seen in the later books of the Old Testament as the divine purpose by which the whole universe is directed. Every man should arrange his life in obedience to that purpose. Wisdom is the plan or intention of God in accordance with which all that went before, and all that comes after, makes sense.

"Christ", says St Paul, "the power of God and the wisdom of God . . . Christ Jesus, whom God made our wisdom" (1 Corinthians 1:24, 30).

●

The Word of God

A word is like a brain-child. A word makes sense of reality. For St John, Jesus is the everlasting Word of God (John 1:1), born of the Father and making sense of our world.

The Word of God does not only exist when it is spoken in our time. Anything existing points to its own eternal existence in God. If there is a word of God, the Word of God, spoken here in time, there must be in God a word eternally conceived. Everything created makes sense only in the light of the one Christ. He is the one Word that must be in God.

A word reflects the mind that speaks it. Jesus is the truth about God, expressed in our flesh.

The one word of human language which perfectly expresses the truth about God is *"Abba!"*

●

"I am called" equals "I was sent"

Think for a few moments about your own vocation. We all have a vocation. God calls each of us, every day. God called me out of nothing when I was conceived; he called me into the light of day when I was born; he called me into a particular childhood and family, to a particular school; he called me through the gifts I have or do not have to the kind of work and life I now have. God calls some to be parents, some to be teachers, some to be healers, doctors and nurses, some to be listeners, some to be talkers, some to be builders, some to be mechanically minded, others to love books, others to have green fingers and make things grow.

There are two sides to the "call" coin. The other side is "sent". I was sent by the Father into the world; I was sent by the Father into the light of day when I was born; I was sent by the Father into a particular childhood and family, to a particular school; he sent me, through the gifts I have or do not have, to the kind of work and life I now have. The Father sends some to be parents, some to be teachers, some to be healers, doctors and nurses, some to be listeners, some to be talkers, some to be builders, some to be mechanically minded, others to love books, others to have green fingers and make things grow.

We too, like Jesus, can truthfully say "The Father has sent me into the world", but that does not mean we were sitting up there outside the world before we were conceived, waiting to be sent.

Jesus is my meaning. I am not his meaning. My call and my mission are tied up in the meaning of Jesus' life, not *vice versa*.

●

When did I become God's child?

Today I know myself as God's child. I was already God's child even before I was baptised. Every child born of woman is a child of God, and christians are those who know and celebrate the fact, as instructed by Jesus. I was born a child of God. I was conceived a child of God. I know all this only because of Jesus, but it is true. I was chosen in Christ before the foundation of the world, and destined in love to be God's son through Jesus Christ.

There is a sense in which you and I have been God's children from all eternity — adopted from all eternity.

●

Sharers in his divinity

By adoption, and not in our own right, we become sharers in the divinity of Christ. So if Christ can say "I and the Father are one", there is a sense in which you and I can say "I and the Father are one". We are one with the Father in Christ, like chicks hidden under Christ's wings.

And yet, being divine as we are, we cannot do all sorts of things philosophy would tell us God can do. We find ourselves weak, as Jesus was, and servants, like him, like his Father.

The "old Adam", the "old Eve", in us wants to be like God (Genesis 3:5) and becomes a servant (cf. Genesis 3:19). The Christ in us wants to be a servant, and becomes like God.

The christian starts along the way following Jesus Christ. Little by little the christian finds himself identified with Jesus Christ, as Jesus uses the christian's eyes to look through, his hands to work. Little by little the christian finds himself (or herself) "one with the Father", since that is what Christ is.

●

The image of God

Man was created in the image of God, in the likeness of God. Christ in whom we are recreated "is the likeness of God" (2 Corinthians 4:4).

An image in a mirror is "one with" the original, but different. A mirror image is just like the original, but it is the-same-back-to-front-and-left-to-right, over against the original. One can look at a mirror image and work out what the reality is like.

A child is "one with" a parent, "one with" both parents, but different. A son who is just like his father is just like his father, but is also related to him.

Jesus is one with the Father. So we can look into Jesus and see what the Father is like. But Jesus is over-against the Father, related to the Father. Jesus is a Son, a child — *the* Son, *the* child, *the* answer, *the* response.

144

Sonship too must be in God. There is nothing good in this world which does not have its origin in God. So reflection, imaging, response, saying "Yes", saying "Thank you", imitating, being like — all these must be in God, in the one Word of God.

The Father is *Abba*. The Son says *"Abba!"* Both are divine.

When we christians in our turn try to be like God, we model ourselves on Jesus; he does not model himself on us. We speak with his Spirit; he does not speak with ours.

●

All things were created through him

"In him all things were created . . . all things were created through him and for him" (Colossians 1:16). Mankind is the crown and glory of creation, and Jesus Christ is the crown and glory of mankind, the one in whom alone we make sense, the one in whom we cry out *"Abba!"* He is the cornerstone of the whole arch of human history, the one in whom alone mankind finds the right approach to God, namely by calling and trusting him as *"Abba!"*

The truth which dawned in Christ had been true from the beginning. His Spirit, and no other, recreates the world, and finally makes sense of the first creation.

●

The Blessed Trinity

The doctrine of the Blessed Trinity is not an extra mystery to be added to all that has been said. This whole booklet has been "about the Trinity".

Like Jesus, you and I are "one with God", "child of God" and "spirit of God". This pattern of relationships corresponds to something in God himself. We go with God, in God, to God. Jesus is our door: he greets every man as a brother, he lives and dies, rises and ascends, and from the Father sends us the Spirit by which we cry out "*Abba! Father!*"

First comes love, making no demands. Then comes acceptance of love by the beloved. The Spirit proceeds from the Father. Then comes love in return, from Son to Father. The Spirit proceeds from the Son, saying "*Abba!*"

The pattern of love which we have discovered in our world thanks to Jesus of Nazareth is to be found in God himself. First comes love, and the beloved disciple believes in it. Then comes love in return. Faith is the beginning, the end is love.

We go with God, in God, to God. Three Persons, one God: "*Abba!*"